Learning Roots

RAMADAN Activity Book

This book belongs to

....

First published in the United Kingdom
in 1440 AH (2019 CE) by
Learning Roots Ltd.
Unit 6, TGEC,
Town Hall Approach Road,
London, N15 4RX
United Kingdom
www.learningroots.com

Editor: Zaheer Khatri
Developed by the Learning Roots
editorial team:
Soulayman Segor, Yasmin Mussa,
Fatima Zahur, Jannah Haque,
Elisa Moriggi, Julia Koschelew and
Muneeba Zahid.

Acknowledgements
The publisher thanks Allāh, Lord of the worlds, for making this publication possible.

British Library Cataloguing in Publication Data
A CIP catalogue record for this book is available from the British Library.

Printed and bound in Turkey.
ISBN: 978-1-905516-79-7

CONTENTS

Explore Ramadan

My First Fasts

Great Deeds

Quran & Dua

Eid Fun

NOTES FOR GROWN-UPS

Is This Book Suitable for Your Child's Age?
This book contains a variety of activities for a suggested age range of 8 years and above. However, please remember that every child is different, and this is just a recommended age range. You will therefore find something suitable for your child's ability as well as extension and support material.

Here's What Your Child Will Learn
The major themes of Ramadan are covered in this book, and are detailed on the contents page. We highly encourage children to experience Ramadan holistically and not just a time when Muslims abstain from food and drink during daylight hours. Above all, Ramadan is about getting closer to Allah, and this is the main message of the book.

This is a (Very) Fun Way to Learn
We believe learning about Islam should be fun and exciting. We've designed these activities in that light and have contextualised the scenarios to reflect this approach.

Each activity contained in this book also promotes the development of one or more key skills, including:

- Spiritual Intelligence
- Creativity
- Fine Motor Skills
- Language Skills
- Problem-Solving
- Thinking Skills
- Observation Skills

The skills related to every activity can be found on each page.

Your Feedback is MORE Than Welcome!
Every effort has been made to ensure the information contained in this pack is accurate, authentic and pedagogically sound. If you find anything to the contrary, we welcome your feedback at: **www.learningroots.com/feedback**

Stickers, Cut-Out & Pull-Out pages
In order to make learning fun and varied, some of the activities in this book require the use of stickers, cut-out objects and pull-out pages. All of these sections are clearly labelled in the book and are referenced on the contents pages. Please ensure you supervise your child when cutting objects from the cut-out pages, or have an adult cut it for them. Similarly, please keep the stickers out of reach from small children under the age of 3 years.

Suggestions on How to Use The Book
We recommend that you spread the activities out across the entire month. Some are designed to be used all month long (such as the calendar activity), while others may be more appropriate at certain times during the month (such as the last 10 nights of Ramadan or Eid). We highly recommend that you **be present to support your child** while they do the activities, in order to foster, create and cherish quality faith-filled moments with your child.

Sharing or Copying Pages from this Book
For the best experience, this publication has been designed to be used by one child. If you would like to use this book with more than one child, such as a large household or a class of children at an educational institution, please purchase one book for every child. Please contact us at **support@learningroots.com** for details on our discounts for educational institutions.

YOUR SHOW GUIDE

Five categories cover the main topics in Ramadan.

Simple reference numbers for you to find your way.

Simple, short and clear instructions that are easy to follow.

Major Ramadan topics are covered to ensure your child gets the essentials plus more.

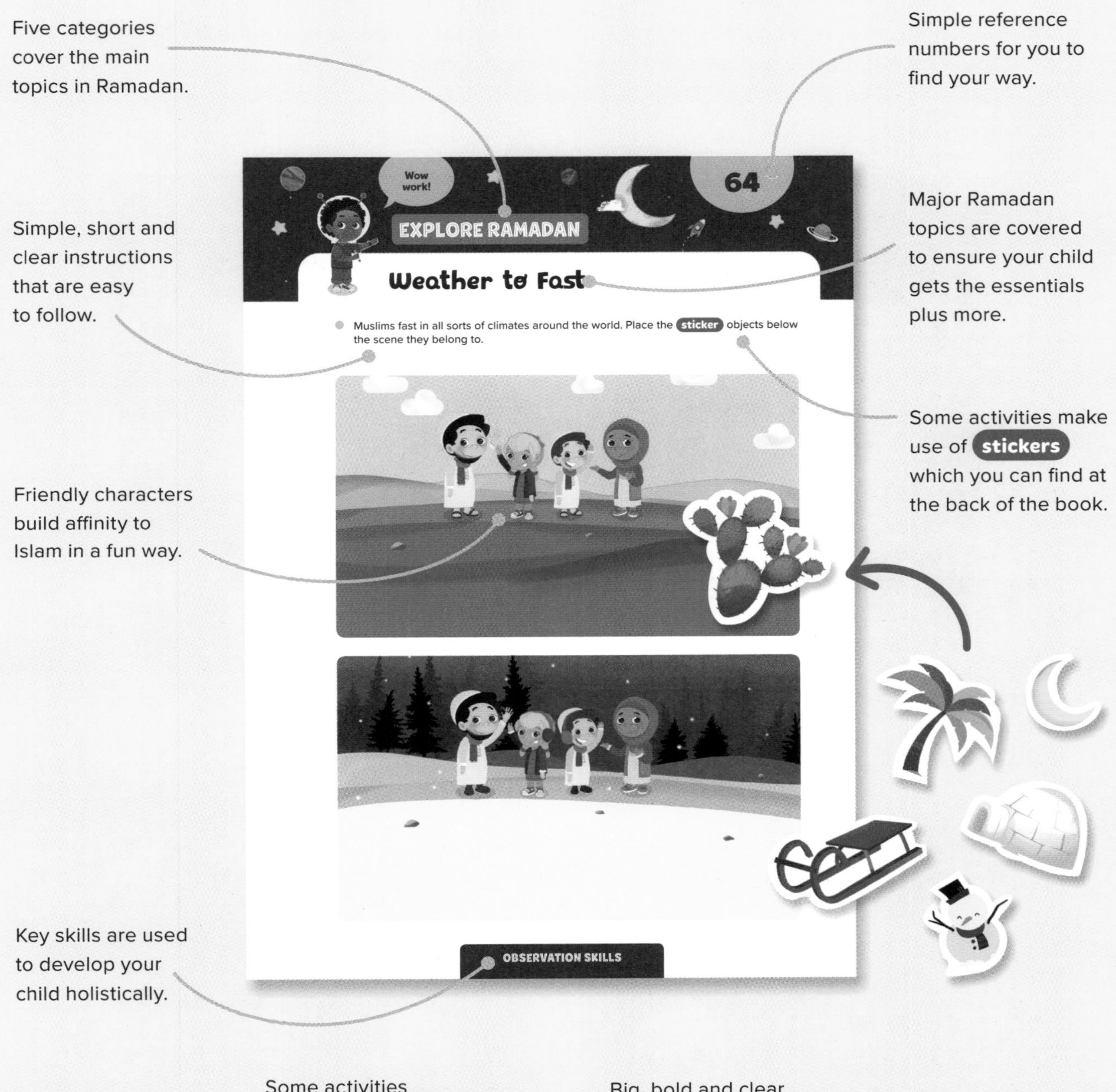

Some activities make use of **stickers** which you can find at the back of the book.

Friendly characters build affinity to Islam in a fun way.

Key skills are used to develop your child holistically.

Some activities require a **grown-up** to help explain or read instructions.

Big, bold and clear activities allow a level of self-controlled play by your child.

Meet the Team

- Match the character names in English with the Arabic names using the **stickers**. You'll be meeting the characters again in the activities to come!

ليث

صفية

زيد

هبة

The Ramadan Story

Start your Ramadan by reading this lovely story with a **grown-up**. It's a must-read!

"The new moon has been spotted!" cheered Daddy, launching his hands in the air.

"*Alhamdulillah*!" said Mummy as she dashed into the living room, and sunk to the floor in *sujood*. Daddy joined her, as the pair sat up and raised their hands in *dua*.

"O Allah! Thank You for giving us this chance again!"

Thabit jumped up from the sofa. He'd never seen his parents like this before. "What's going on Mummy and Daddy? What's this chance all about?"

Daddy stood up and wrapped his arms around Thabit. Mummy sat up on the sofa and the pair joined her. Both parents looked their son in the eyes. "Thabit," said Mummy, "the great month of Ramadan starts tonight. It's a month in which Allah has made fasting a must, and prayer during its nights a way for us to draw closer to Him."

Thabit looked a little confused. "What does fasting mean? Is that when you run really quickly?" Daddy chuckled.

"Not quite," he said. "Fasting is when we don't eat or drink during the whole day, from the early morning at *Fajr*, until the evening at *Maghrib*."

"Not even a sip of water?" asked Thabit.

"Not even a crumb of a cookie," said Mummy. "And we do that for a whole month."

"But why? Why do we have to do that?" asked Thabit.

"Because Allah has told us to. And Allah knows best," said Daddy. "Besides, fasting makes your mind, body and heart stronger. It teaches you control, patience and giving things up for Allah's sake."

"So it's kind of like training then," said Thabit.

"Kind of, but the school of Ramadan carries on into the night."

"What do you mean?"

"You see, fasting makes your heart softer, and so you love to worship Allah more. That's why there are extra prayers at night."

"But why Ramadan? What's so special about this month?" asked Thabit.

"Because in Ramadan, the gates of *Jannah* are opened, the gates of *Jahannam* are closed and Shaytan is locked up. And in this month, the Quran came down to the Prophet Muhammad ﷺ."

"Ah..I see!"

"It came down on a night called '*Laylatul Qadr*'—the Night of Power," explained Daddy.

"How much power did Allah put into that night?"

"Power that's better than one thousand months!"

Thabit's mouth gaped open. His eyes widened in awe. "A thousand months?!"

"A thousand months indeed!" said Mummy.

"I definitely don't want to miss that night Mummy! Please wake me up so I can catch some of that power."

"I will do *in-sha-Allah*."

"It's a shame Ramadan is only a month long. I wish it could last longer!"

Mummy smiled, "At the end of Ramadan we'll have a day of Eid."

"What's Eid?"

"Eid is a day to mark the end of Ramadan with a special prayer, giving in charity, meeting our family and friends, oh and of course..." Mummy raised her eyebrows.

"Of course what Mummy?" asked Thabit as a smile spread across his face.

"Presents, Thabit. Presents!"

You're all set!

Your Get-Set Calendar

- Follow the steps below to set up your own Ramadan calendar. Then use the calendar every day to track your Ramadan goals.

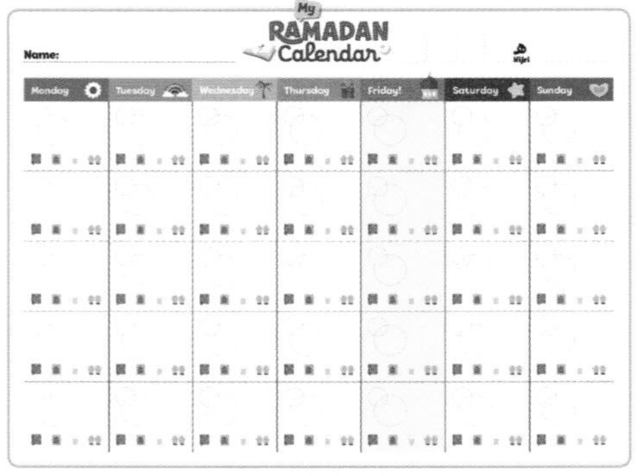

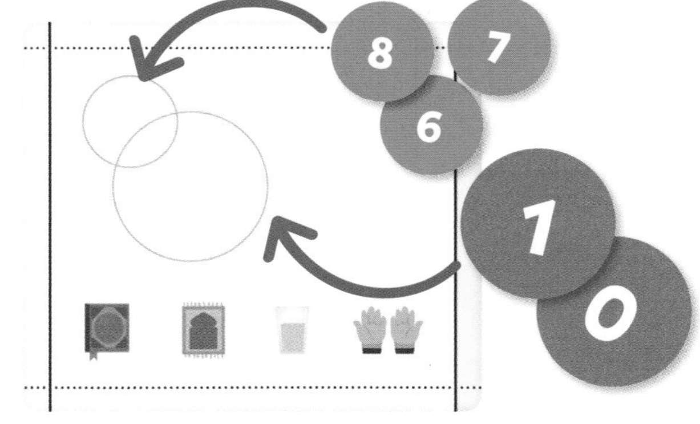

1 Find the pull-out calendar in this book and carefully tear it off. Write your name at the top of the calendar and use the **stickers** to enter the Islamic and Gregorian years.

2 Next, fill in the days of Ramadan and the days of the Gregorian months as shown using the **stickers** provided. If there's not enough room at the end, continue on to the first row again.

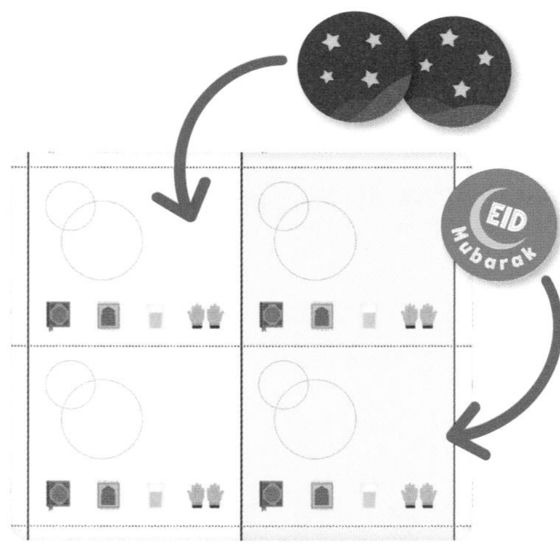

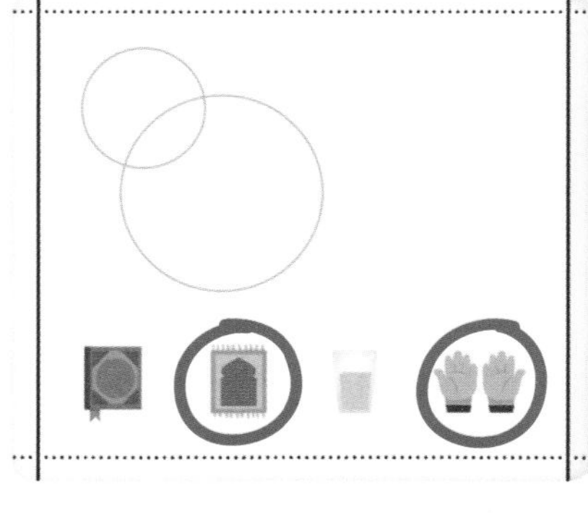

Use your calendar every day!

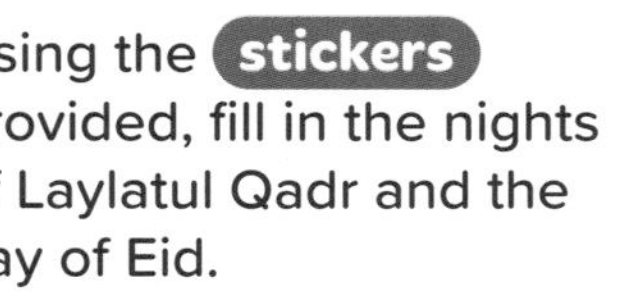

3 Using the **stickers** provided, fill in the nights of Laylatul Qadr and the day of Eid.

4 Set yourself a goal this Ramadan and mark your progress on the calendar. Your goal can be something simple like memorising one line of the Quran every day!

That's a nice banner!

Ramadan Mubarak!

- Make your very own Ramadan Mubarak banner by following the steps below.

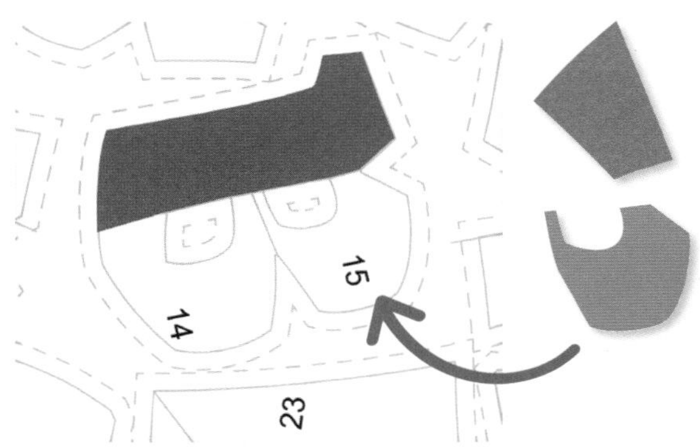

1 Find the banner letters in the cut-out section. Then use the **stickers** to match and fill the zones in the letters. Your letters will look beautiful after you've finished!

2 Next, cut each letter out using scissors. If you wish, you can mount the cut-outs on card before cutting them out.

RAMADAN
& EID
MUBARAK

3 Choose a suitable area on a wall in your home and stick the letters up using blue-tac or another suitable adhesive.

Pillar Puzzle

- Tick the five pillars of Islam from the images below. Use the *hadeeth* to help you find them.

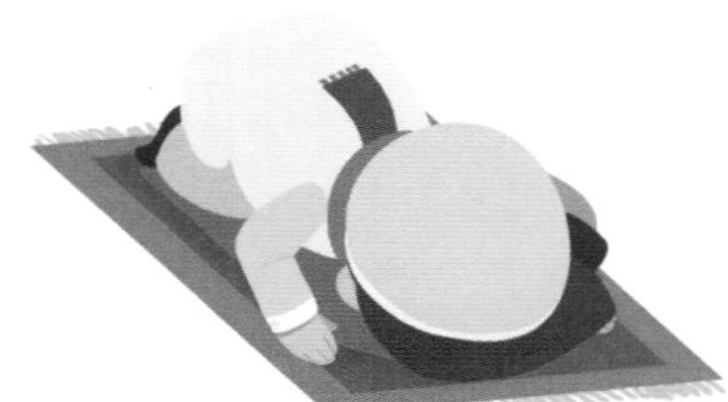

○ **Establishing the Prayer**

○ **Fasting Ramadan**

○ **Testimony of Faith**

○ **Reciting Quran**

○ **Giving Zakah**

○ **Hajj**

The Prophet ﷺ said:

“ *Islam has been built on five (pillars): testifying that there is no one worthy of worship except Allah and that Muhammad is the Messenger of Allah, establishing the prayer, paying the Zakah, making the Hajj to the House, and fasting Ramadan. (Bukhari & Muslim)*

From Suhoor to Dawn

- Number the pictures in order to figure out Thabit's Ramadan morning routine, then write a sentence explaining each scene.

Is it time yet?

- Tick one picture that shows that the time for *maghrib* has started so that Sarah can break her fast.

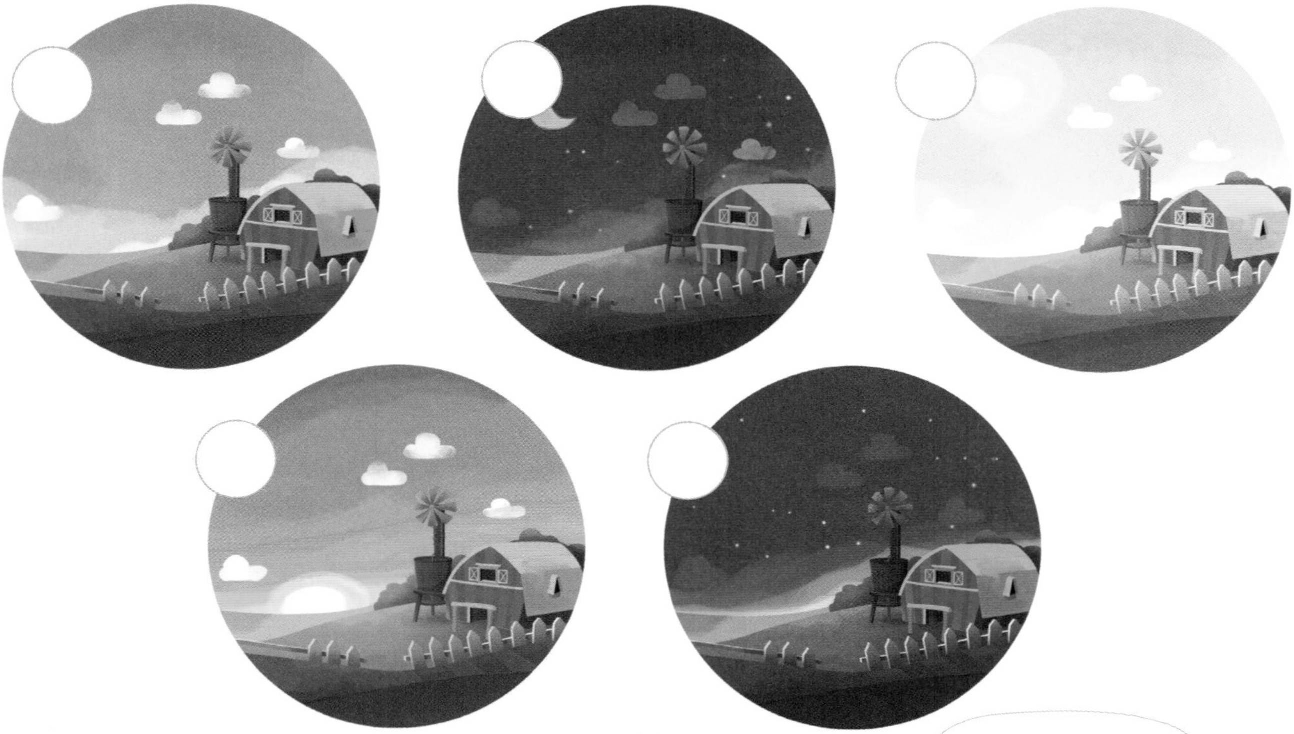

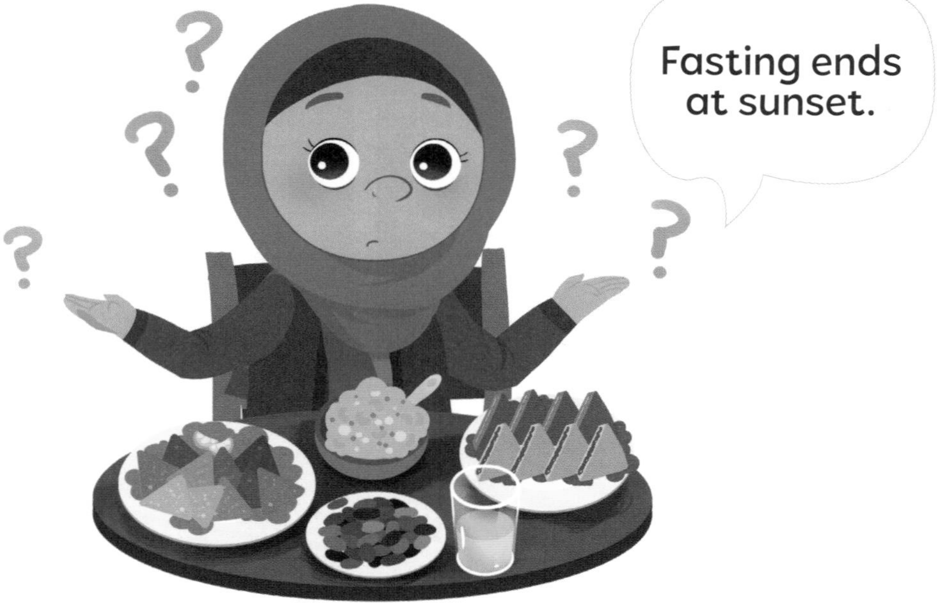

Fasting ends at sunset.

GREAT DEEDS

Wudu Splash

- Match the **stickers** to the body parts Qays needs to wash when he makes *wudu*. Then number the parts in the correct order of *wudu*.

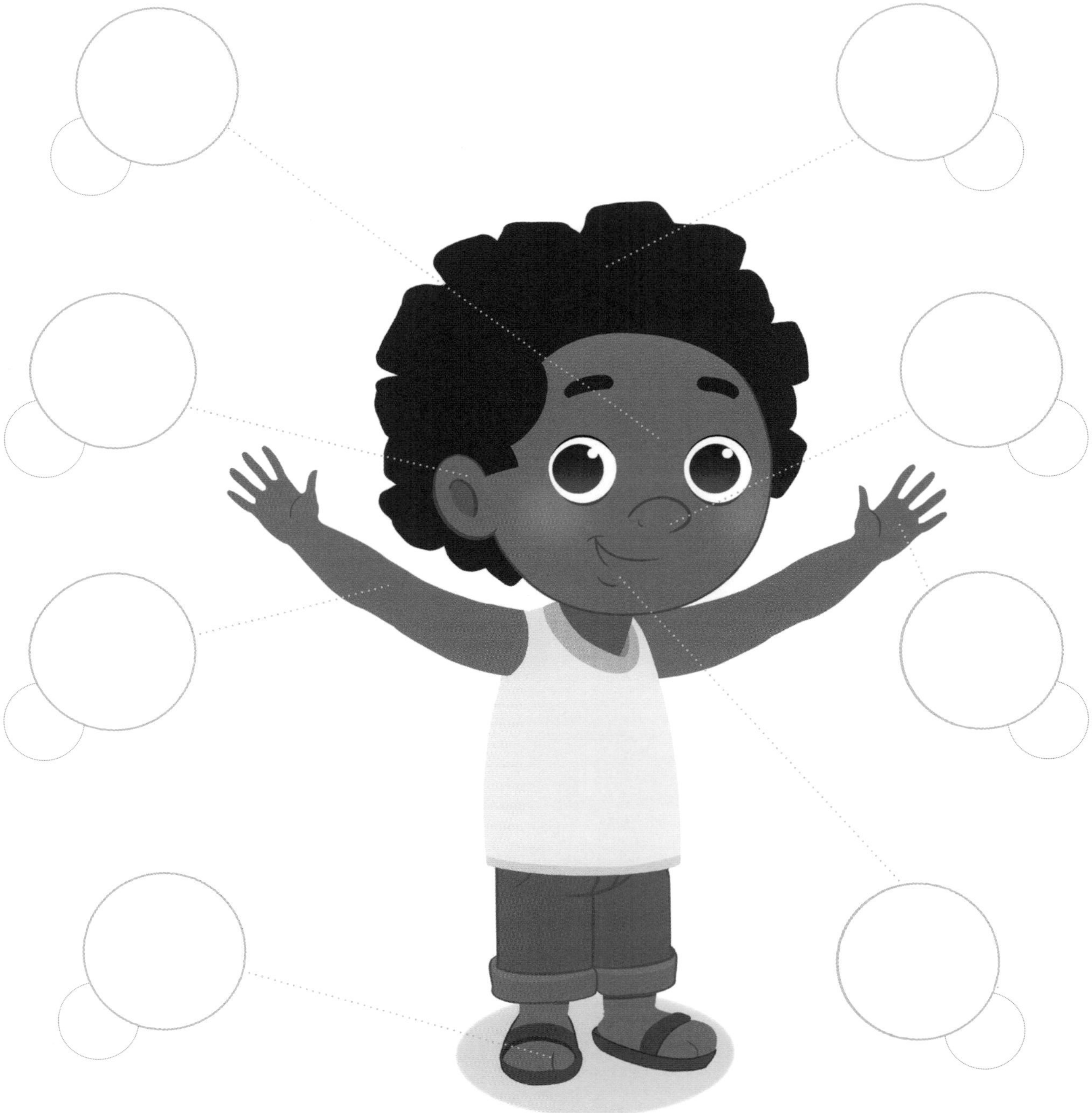

GREAT DEEDS

Prayer Positions

- Match the picture of each prayer position to its name.

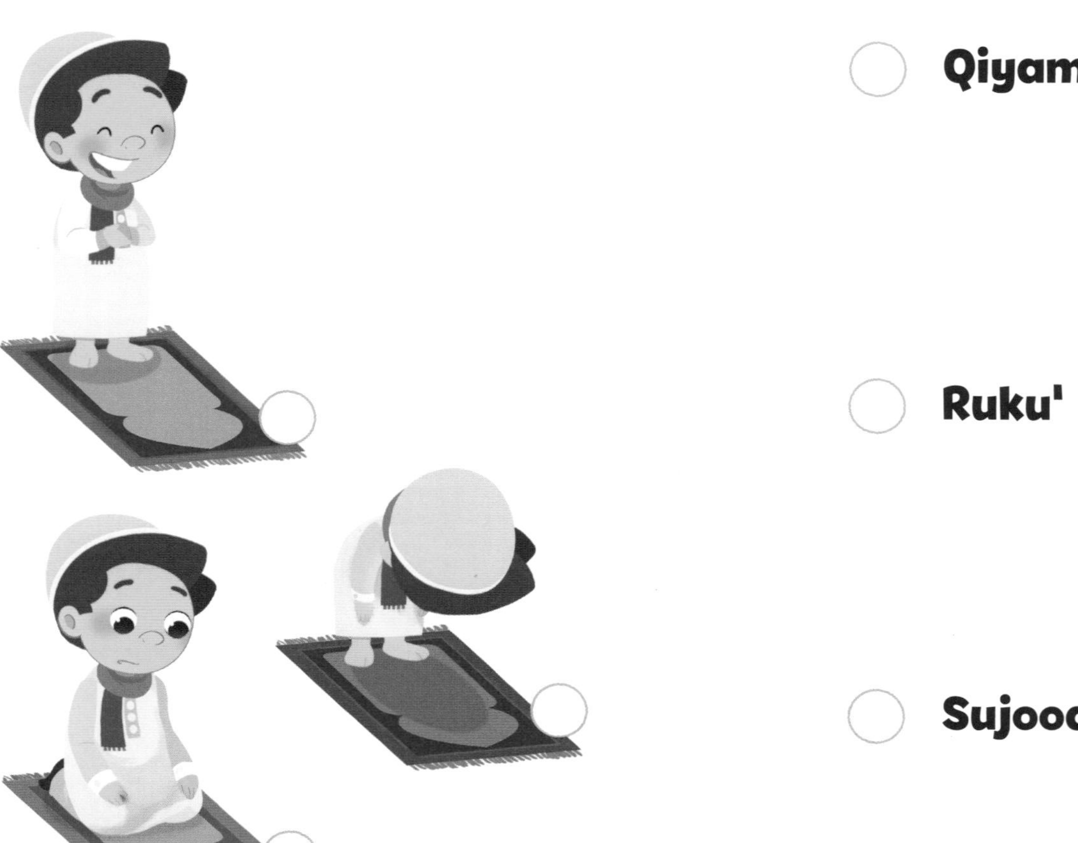

- Qiyam
- Ruku'
- Sujood
- Takbiratul-Ihram
- Tashahud

Who Am I?

- Which boy is doing all of the following actions:
  Reciting *Surah An-Naas* **and** wearing a buttoned thobe **and** sitting on a mat containing the colour blue? Tick the right character and cross out the others.

Monthly Clues

- Help Qays to put the Islamic months in order using the clues below. He's done one example for you.

- **Muharram** is in the same position in the Islamic calendar as January is in the Gregorian calendar.
- **Ramadan** is the ninth month in the Islamic calendar.
- **Dhul-Hijjah** is the third month after **Ramadan**, and comes after the month of **'Dhul Qa'dah.**
- **Safar** is the month between **Muharram** and **Rabi'ul-Awwal**.
- **Rajab** comes before **Sha'ban**, which comes before **Ramadan**.
- Eid Al-Fitr is in the month of **Shawwal**.
- **Jumadal-Ulaa** comes before **Jumadal-Akhirah** and both of these months come after **Rabi'ul-Thani**.

1. ....
2. **Safar**
3. ....
4. ....
5. ....
6. ....
7. ....
8. ....
9. ....
10. ....
11. ....
12. ....

From Iftar to Sleep

- Number the pictures in order to figure out Thabit's Ramadan evening routine, then write a sentence explaining each scene.

Table Manners

- Match the **stickers** to the correct speech bubbles and then order the steps Thabit takes when breaking his fast.

Salah Match

- Using the key to help you, show the type and number of each unit of prayer for the five daily prayers. Thabit has done one example for you.

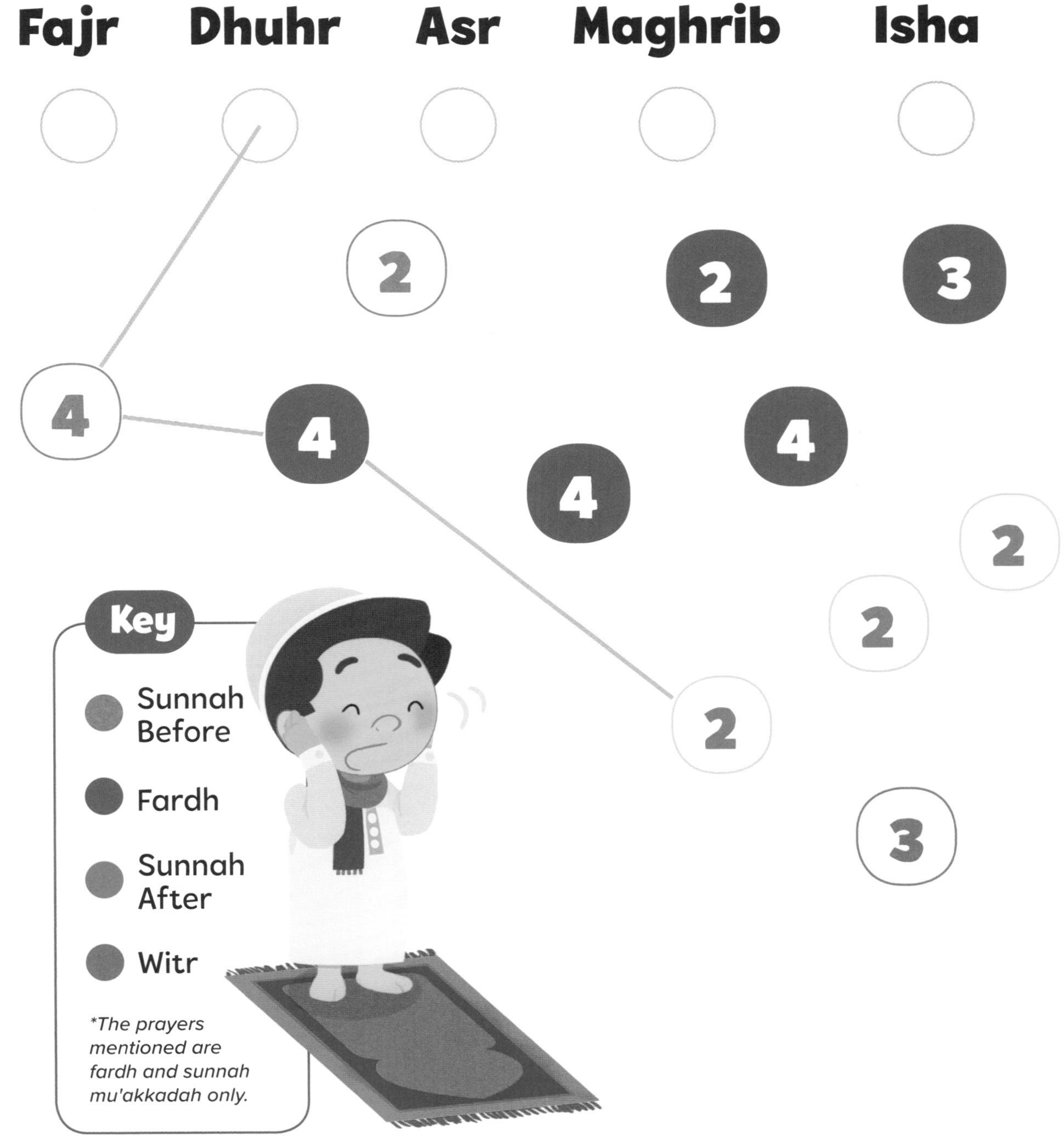

QURAN AND DUA

Page Turner

- Add up the boxes for each character to find out who has read the most Quran pages today. You'll need to find out what the Arabic numbers stand for by using the key below.

Key

0	1	2	3	4	5	6	7	8	9
٠	١	٢	٣	٤	٥	٦	٧	٨	٩

Hiba

٢ + ٦ + ٥ = ...

....

Thabit

٨ + ٤ + ٣ = ...

....

Aisha

٧ + ٩ + ١ = ...

....

Well Mannered

- Spot the six differences between the pictures below that show Qays helping his friend carry a box.

A Day in Ramadan

- Label each activity in Ramadan using **stickers**. Explain what's happening in each event to a **grown-up**.

Iftar Party

- Spot 6 difference between the two trays Sarah has prepared for her guests.

Never-Ending Charity

- Sarah lives in London and would like to give her money to a local cause that will help poor children. Choose, from the options below, the cause that best fits Sarah's intention.

African Wells

We build water wells in the areas of drought in Africa.

Capital Orphans

We care for orphans in the United Kingdom's capital city.

Homeless Palace

We feed the homeless at Buckingham Palace in London.

Syrian Care

We help the Syrian refugees around the world.

Animal Adventures

- Match the Quran *surah* names to the correct English meaning.

Baqarah سورة البقرة	**Elephant**
Nahl سورة النحل	**Spider**
Naml سورة النمل	**Cow**
Feel سورة الفيل	**Ant**
Ankaboot سورة العنكبوت	**Bee**

Use the surah titles to find the meanings from the Quran!

Excellent work!

Month Detective

- Complete the word search of the Islamic months. Ramadan has been found for you.

G	S	R	X	F	S	N	W	Z	G	O	V	P	U	G	X
P	D	M	U	H	A	R	R	A	M	W	A	K	A	D	S
P	S	D	A	T	U	J	W	C	O	P	U	Q	Y	H	A
J	O	S	F	X	L	Q	U	W	C	Q	B	Z	A	V	F
J	M	P	H	S	G	R	U	U	X	V	U	R	U	U	A
U	S	Q	L	A	R	E	Y	N	I	D	I	N	Z	K	R
M	A	H	R	A	B	I	U	L	T	H	A	N	I	A	S
A	F	J	A	T	L	A	Q	R	K	U	P	W	Z	H	D
D	F	P	M	W	K	S	N	A	L	L	M	P	I	U	H
A	X	D	A	B	W	I	L	E	Z	H	B	I	C	U	U
L	U	K	D	P	N	A	Z	C	A	I	Y	N	V	L	L
U	O	Z	A	B	D	O	L	V	E	J	R	Q	I	G	Q
L	Y	T	N	A	N	U	Q	O	O	J	X	N	R	I	A
A	G	N	M	P	F	Y	P	E	R	A	F	V	B	N	D
A	L	U	R	A	J	A	B	C	C	H	V	B	N	J	A
J	J	P	R	A	B	I	U	L	A	W	W	A	L	R	H

1. **Muharram**
2. **Safar**
3. **Rabiulawwal**
4. **Rabiulthani**
5. **Jumadalulaa**
6. **Jumadalakhirah**
7. **Rajab**
8. **Shaban**
9. **Ramadan**
10. **Shawwal**
11. **Dhulqadah**
12. **Dhulhijjah**

You're So Special!

- Match the virtues of Ramadan to their images. Use the *hadeeth* to fill in the missing virtues before matching them.

Forgiveness for Fasting

Quran Revealed

Escape from the Hell-Fire

Contains Laylatul Qadr

The Prophet ﷺ said:

When Ramadan comes, the gates of Paradise are opened, the gates of Hell are closed, and the devils are chained up. (Bukhari)

Right Hand Side

- Aisha uses her right hand to do good things like reading Quran, eating or shaking hands. Study the pictures below and circle her right hand in each pose.

1

2

3

4

5

6

Sincere Dua

- Label each child's dua with the number of the Arabic versions below using the Arabic keywords to help you.

I made dua for Paradise.

الْجَنَّةَ

النَّارِ

I made dua to be saved from the Fire.

I made dua for my salah and fasting to be accepted.

صَلَاتِي

وَلِوَالِدَيَّ

I made dua for myself and my parent's forgiveness.

1 اللّٰهُمَّ إِنِّي أَعُوذُ بِكَ مِنَ النَّارِ

2 اللّٰهُمَّ تَقَبَّلْ صَلَاتِي وَصِيَامِي

3 اللّٰهُمَّ إِنِّي أَسْأَلُكَ الْجَنَّةَ

4 اللّٰهُمَّ اغْفِرْ لِي وَلِوَالِدَيَّ

Busy Nights

- Find the items in the list that Zayd will need to make the most of his Ramadan nights.

Prayer Mat
Quran
Alarm Clock
Water Bottle
Clock
Dates
Calendar

1 2 3 4 5
6 7 8

QURAN

The Sun and the Moon

- Read the passage below to learn about the differences between lunar and solar years. Use what you've learnt to answer the questions below.

The Islamic calendar is based on a lunar year, which is the time it takes for 12 full moon phases. One of the great things about the lunar calendar is that you can tell the day of the month by just looking at the moon. For example, a full moon means it's the 15th day of the month.

You can't do that with a solar calendar. That's the calendar that most countries use in the world today and is based on the time is takes for the earth to go around the sun. In a solar calendar, the seasons stay the same in every month throughout the year.

Like the Prophet ﷺ said, a lunar month is either 29 or 30 days which means a lunar year is shorter than a solar year by about 10 days. That's why Ramadan moves between different seasons.

1. **What's one advantage of the lunar calendar?**

   ....

   ....

2. **What's one advantage of the solar calendar?**

   ....

   ....

3. **As the years go by, why does Ramadan occur in different seasons?**

   ....

   ....

It's About Time

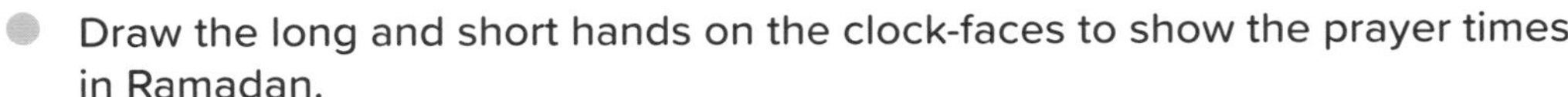

- Draw the long and short hands on the clock-faces to show the prayer times in Ramadan.

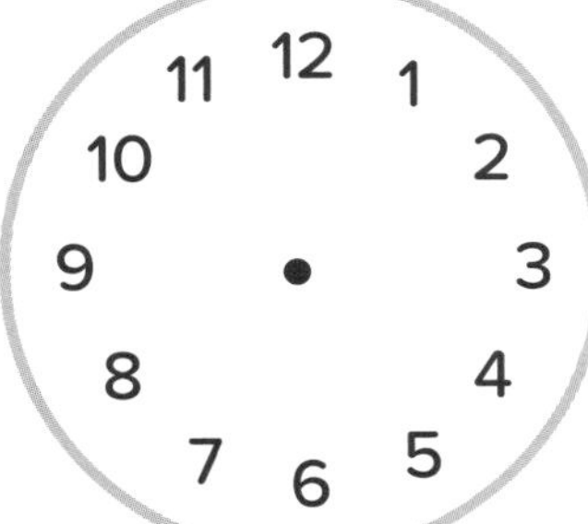

5:30
Suhoor Ends & Fajr

1:00
Zuhr

4:00
Asr

The prayer times will be different in your town!

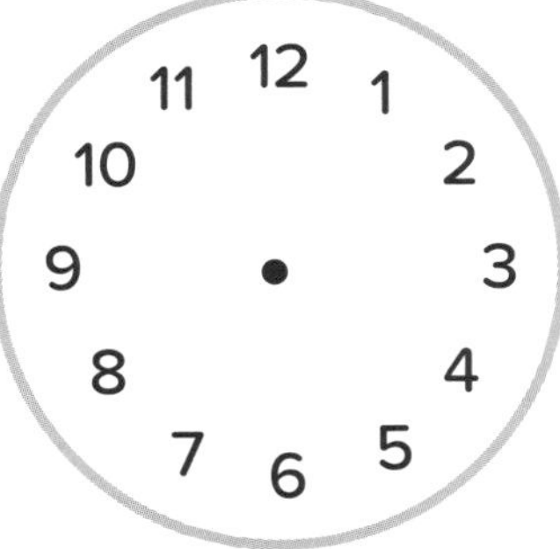

6:15
Maghrib & Iftar

7:45
Isha then Tarawih

No Time to Lose!

Help Qays reach home for iftar as fast as possible without taking your pencil off the road. Note your times in the box below. What's your fastest time?

Time

Masjid Manners

- Circle the people that are doing things that they should **not** be doing in the masjid. Explain to a **grown-up** why some of the actions don't seem right.

Charity

Not Now...

- Below are times when it's **not** allowed to fast. However, there's one mistake. Use the *hadeeth* to find it and cross it out.

Eid ul-Adha

Night Before Ramadan

3 Days of Tashreeq

WED

Wednesdays

Eid ul-Fitr

The Prophet ﷺ said:

Do not anticipate Ramadan by fasting one or two days before it begins, but if someone normally fasts (in that pattern), then let them fast. (Bukhari) • Do not fast on these days (3 days after Eid ul-Adha) for they are the days of eating and drinking. (Saheeh al-Jami')

I'm Off to Makkah!

Use the **stickers** to label Masjid Al-Haram according to the key provided.

1. Hajr Aswad (Black Stone)
2. Maqaam–Ibrahim
3. Door of the Kabah
4. Ghilaaf (Cover of the Kabah)
5. Mataaf (Tawaaf Area)
6. Hateem (Semi-Circle area)

This is a great tool!

Moon Moves

- Make a moon date-finder by following the steps below. You'll need the finder for the next page!

1. Find the moon date-finder in the cut-out section. Next, cut both shapes out using scissors. If you wish, you can mount the cut-outs on card. You should ask a **grown-up** to you help you.

2. Use a split-pin to pierce a hole in the middle of each circle and attach the two pieces together.

3. Spread out the two ends of the split pin and the moon date-finder should now spin freely to help you find the date of each moon-phase.

- With the help of the moon date -finder you've made, fill in the dates in the passage below. Use the images to help you.

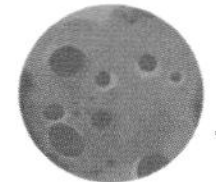

Fasting begins on the ....st of Ramadan.

The ....th marks the end of the first third of the month.

By the ....th of the month, half of Ramadan has already passed, and the last .... nights are ones in which the Night of Power is found.

Some people put all their efforts in worshipping on the ....th night, but really, Laylatul Qadr can fall on any of the odd nights after the ....th of Ramadan.

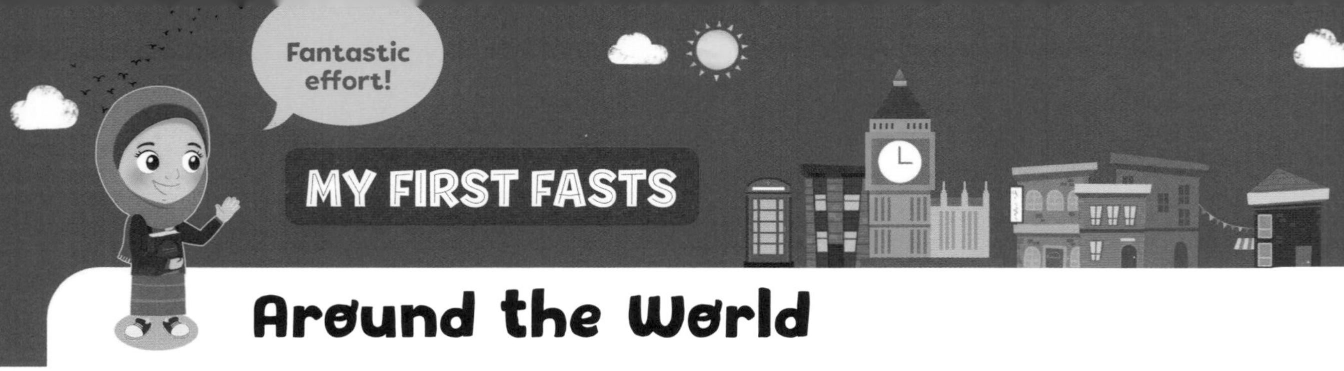

Around the World

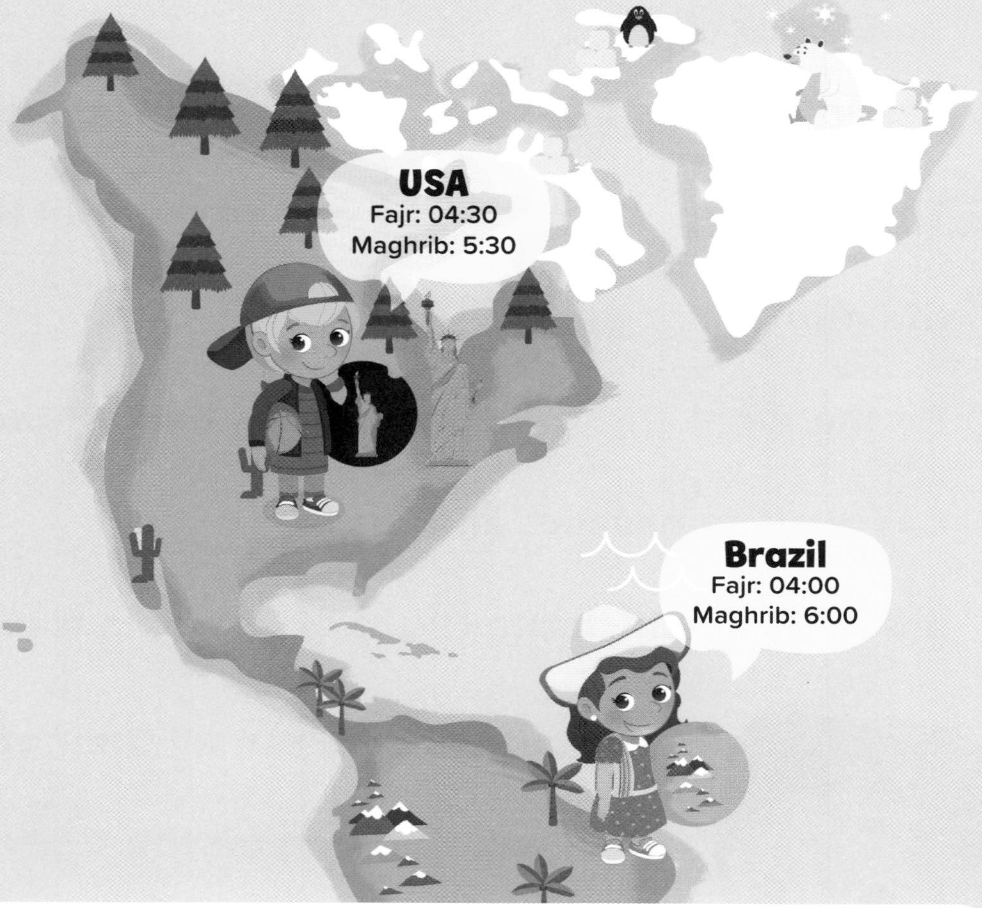

USA
Fajr: 04:30
Maghrib: 5:30

Brazil
Fajr: 04:00
Maghrib: 6:00

Use the information on the map to answer these questions:

1. What time is Fajr in South America?

   ……………………………………………

2. When is Maghrib in Australia?

   ……………………………………………

3. How long is the fast in Africa?

   ……………………………………… Hours

4. How much shorter is the fast in China compared to North America?

   ……………………………………… Hours

5. Which country has the longest fast?

   ……………………………………………

UK
Fajr: 03:30
Maghrib: 8:30

China
Fajr: 05:00
Maghrib: 5:30

Kenya
Fajr: 04:30
Maghrib: 5:30

Australia
Fajr: 06:30
Maghrib: 5:00

Who Sees You?

- Number the four story images on this page in order, then answer the questions below.

When he thought no one was looking, Musa gobbled down a cookie.

Musa kept quiet about what had happened and joined his family at *iftar* time.

It's Ramadan and Musa is having a go at fasting his first full day. He rose early for *suhoor* with his family.

While at school, Musa's stomach groaned in hunger.

1 Did anyone see Musa eat the cookie?

....

2 Should Musa have told his parents about the cookie?

....

- Number the four story images on this page in order, then answer the questions below.

Musa raised his hands to Allah, asked for forgiveness and thanked Allah for the lesson he learnt that day.

Musa's parents comforted him. They disliked Musa's secret, but they were happy he showed the courage to tell them the truth.

Knowing that he could not hide anything from Allah, Musa told his parents what happened.

Late at night, Musa's mind couldn't rest. Even if no one saw him, surely Allah sees everything.

1. **Why did Musa tell his parents about the cookie?**

   ....

2. **How do you think Musa felt after making dua to Allah?**

   ....

Peace of the Masjid

- Spot six differences between the masjid scenes in which Team Ramadan is doing itikaf.

Itikaf is when you stay in the masjid for a few days to worship Allah.

For the First Time...

- Write about the experience of your first fast. How did you feel? What is easier or harder than you thought? Did you feel closer to Allah afterwards? Use the word box to give you some ideas.

close to Allah **grateful**
higher iman **sleepy** **tired**
worried **hungry**
happy **energetic** **brave**

Remind Me in Ramadan

- Ramadan is a great time to practice, repeat and master new words to remember Allah. In this activity, you'll memorise some really powerful words that will earn you lots of rewards!

Cut out the 'Remind Me' shapes from the cut-out section at the back of the book.

Find a suitable space on a wall in your house to stick the reminders on.

Each time you pass by the reminder, recite the words on there and repeat after them. You'll soon learn the words by heart!

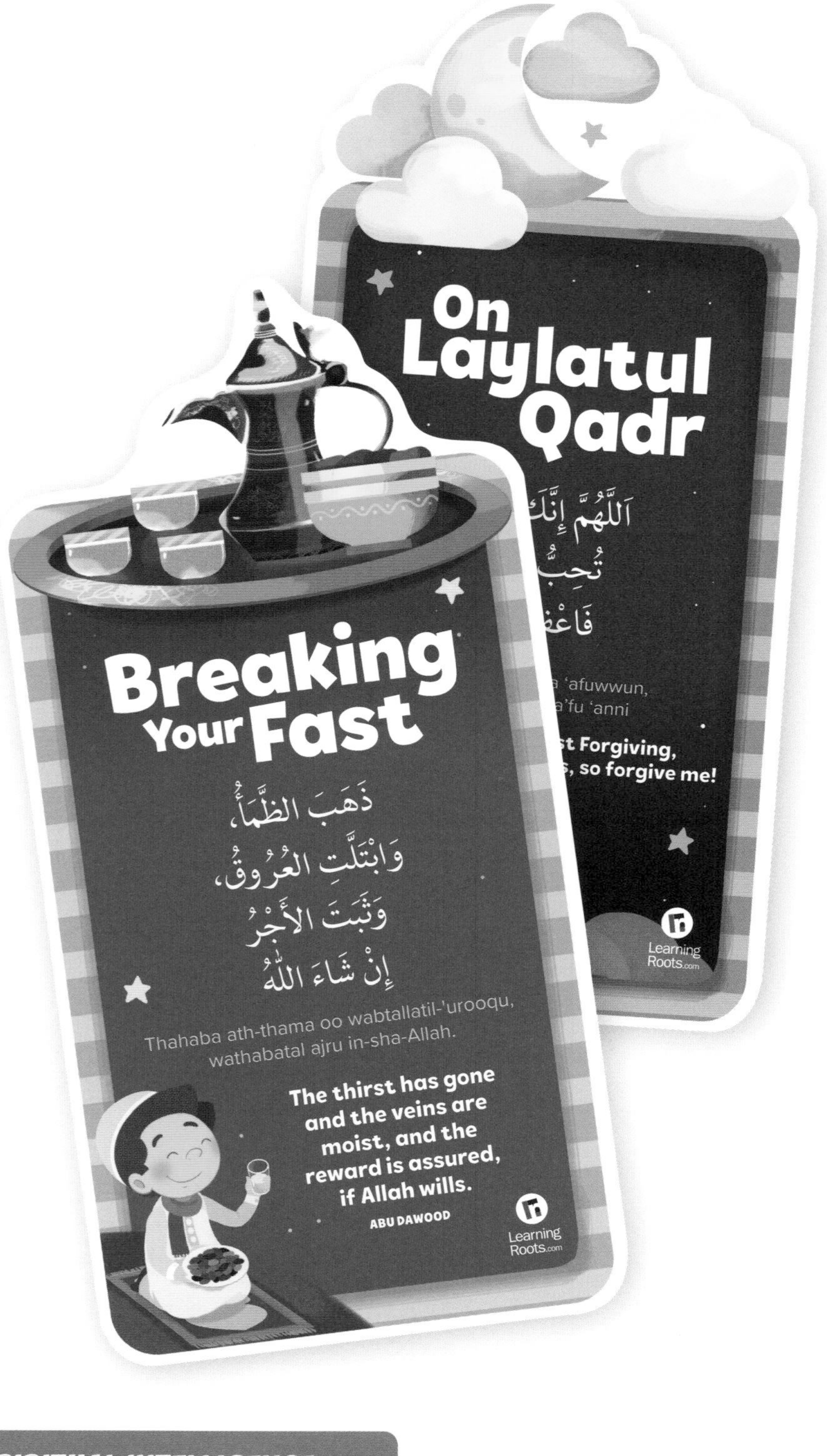

On Laylatul Qadr

Breaking Your Fast

ذَهَبَ الظَّمَأُ،
وَابْتَلَّتِ الْعُرُوقُ،
وَثَبَتَ الأَجْرُ
إِنْ شَاءَ اللَّهُ

Thahaba ath-thama oo wabtallatil-'urooqu, wathabatal ajru in-sha-Allah.

The thirst has gone and the veins are moist, and the reward is assured, if Allah wills.

ABU DAWOOD

LearningRoots.com

Happy Habits

- Tick the things Thabit could do more of to make the most of his time in the special month of Ramadan. Can you explain to a **grown-up** why these habits are good or not so good?

Fast Finder

- Find the word 'Ramadan' in Arabic.

رمضان

راكض

ثابت

راضعة

حوض

رضاء

زمان

رياح

زيارة

رباعي

زياد

رملة

زمزم

رماح

روح

روضة

رياض

ريعان

رضاعة

رملة

حصان

مبين

رجفان

زيد

بيان

رمضان

زبائن

In salah is peace!

GREAT DEEDS

Prayer Focus

- Tick the thoughts that Thabit should focus on during the prayer, and cross out the ones he should try **not** to think about.

Dua Manners

- Follow the three steps below to write your own *dua*. Look at the examples of each character, but don't copy them!

Praise and Thank Allah

Send Salutations Upon the Prophet Muhammad ﷺ

Ask for Your Wishes in this World and the Next

O Allah! How perfect You are! All praise belongs to you!

O Allah! Send Your peace and blessings upon the Prophet Muhammad!

O Allah! I ask you for the best in the dunya and the aakhira!

1 ....

2 ....

3 ....

Words Apart

- Join the words to make a Ramadan phrase. Aisha has done one example for you.

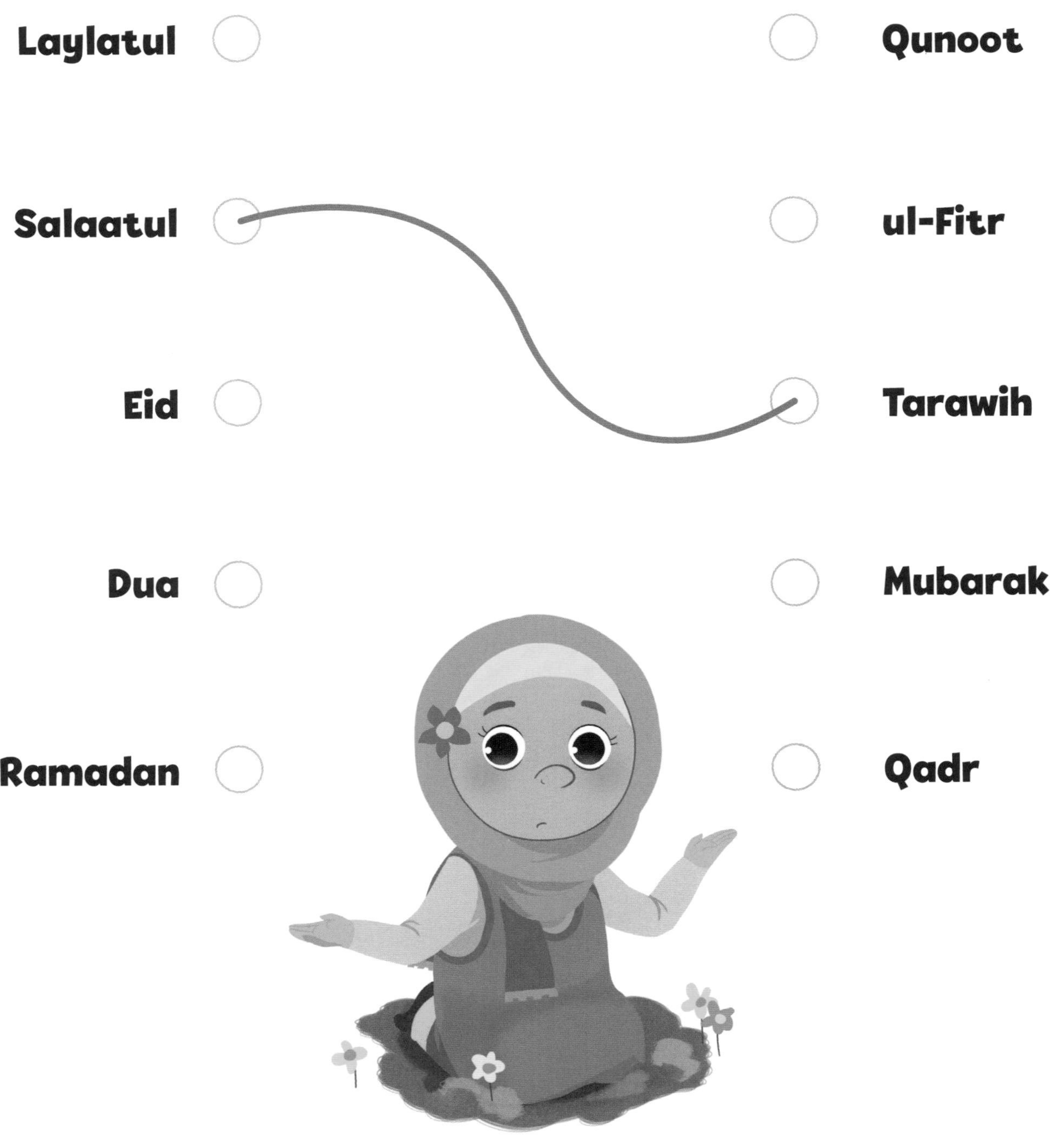

A Blessed Meal

- Tick whether these statements are true or false. If they're false, correct them in the space provided.

	True	False	
There's a special *barakah* (blessing) in having the *suhoor* meal.	◯	◯	....
If you fast without having suhoor, your fast doesn't count.	◯	◯	....
It's best to have the suhoor meal as late as possible.	◯	◯	....
It's not a good idea to drink water at suhoor time.	◯	◯	....
It's best to over-eat at suhoor time so that our tummies are full for the day.	◯	◯	....

GREAT DEEDS

Give to Get

- Study each picture carefully and answer the questions below.

1. Below the line in the circle next to each character, write down how much money each character has. Who has the most money overall?

   ....

2. Now, above the line in each circle, write down how much each character has given in charity. Who has given the most money?

   ....

3. You've now written a fraction in the circle! With the help of a grown-up work out who has given the most money compared to what they had.

   ....

Code Buster

- Using the key to help you, match each symbol to an Arabic letter to reveal an Arabic word. What does it say?

....

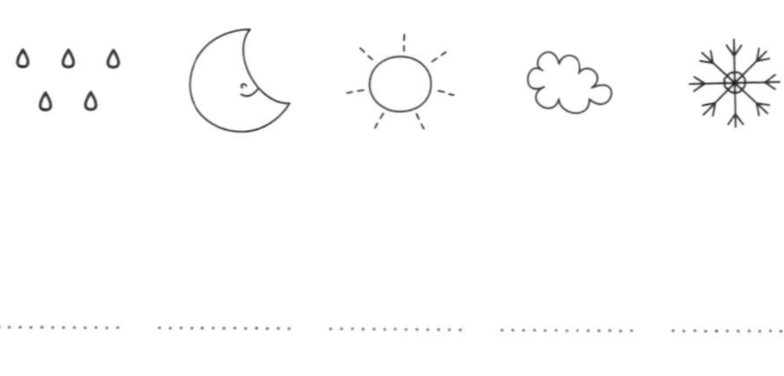

....

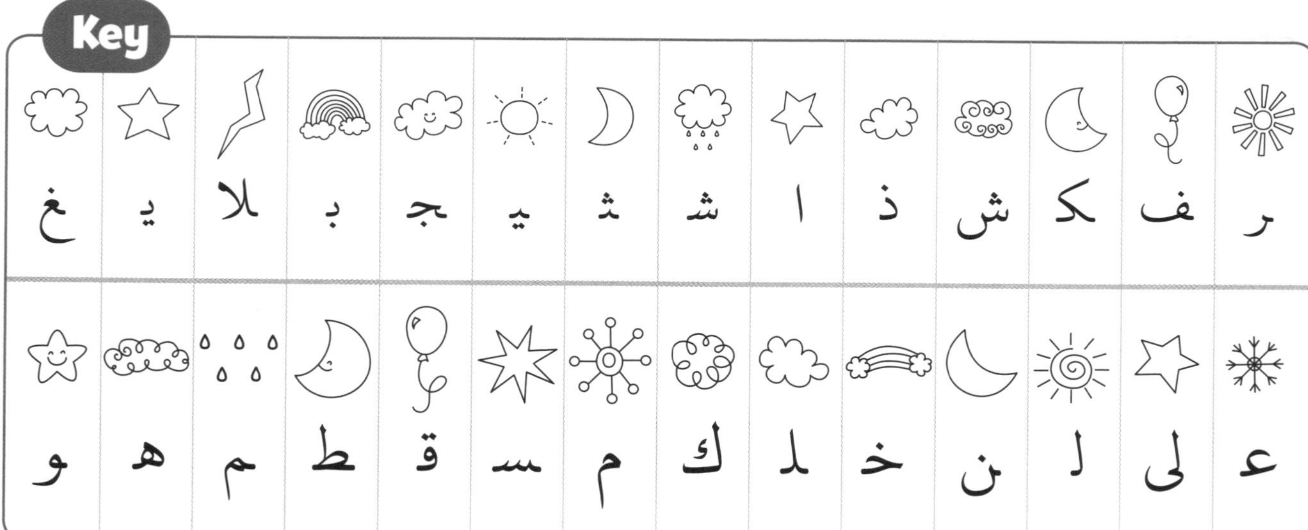

Such a great reader!

Historical Fun

- Read the scroll on the history of Ramadan and use what you've learnt to answer the questions below.

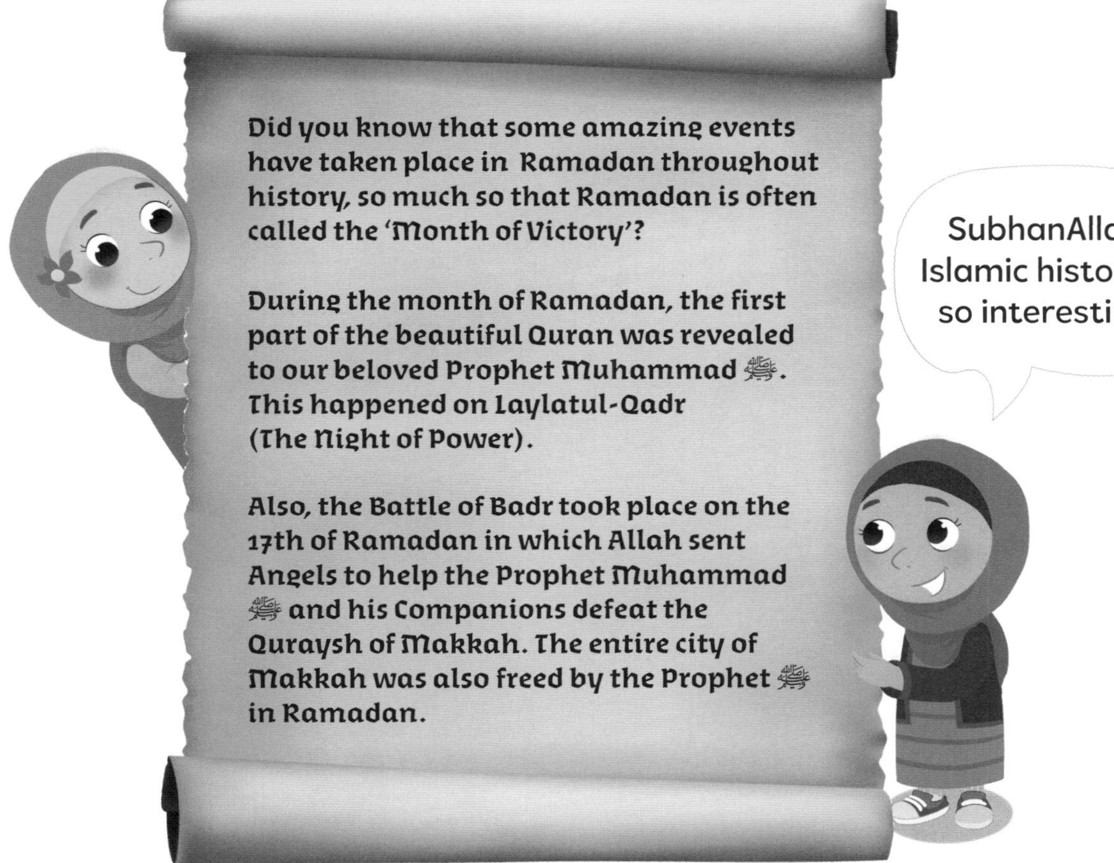

1. **Which book was revealed in Ramadan?**

   ....

2. **What's the name of the special night in Ramadan?**

   ....

3. **Who did Allah send down in the Battle of Badr?**

   ....

4. **Why is Ramadan also called the 'Month of Victory'?**

   ....

Break Fast

- Figure out and re-write what Aisha and her friends are saying about actions that do not break the fast.

1 ....

2 ....

3 ....

Leaving Nicely

Help Thabit reach the exit. He cannot walk in front of someone praying without a *sutrah* (barrier) in front of them.

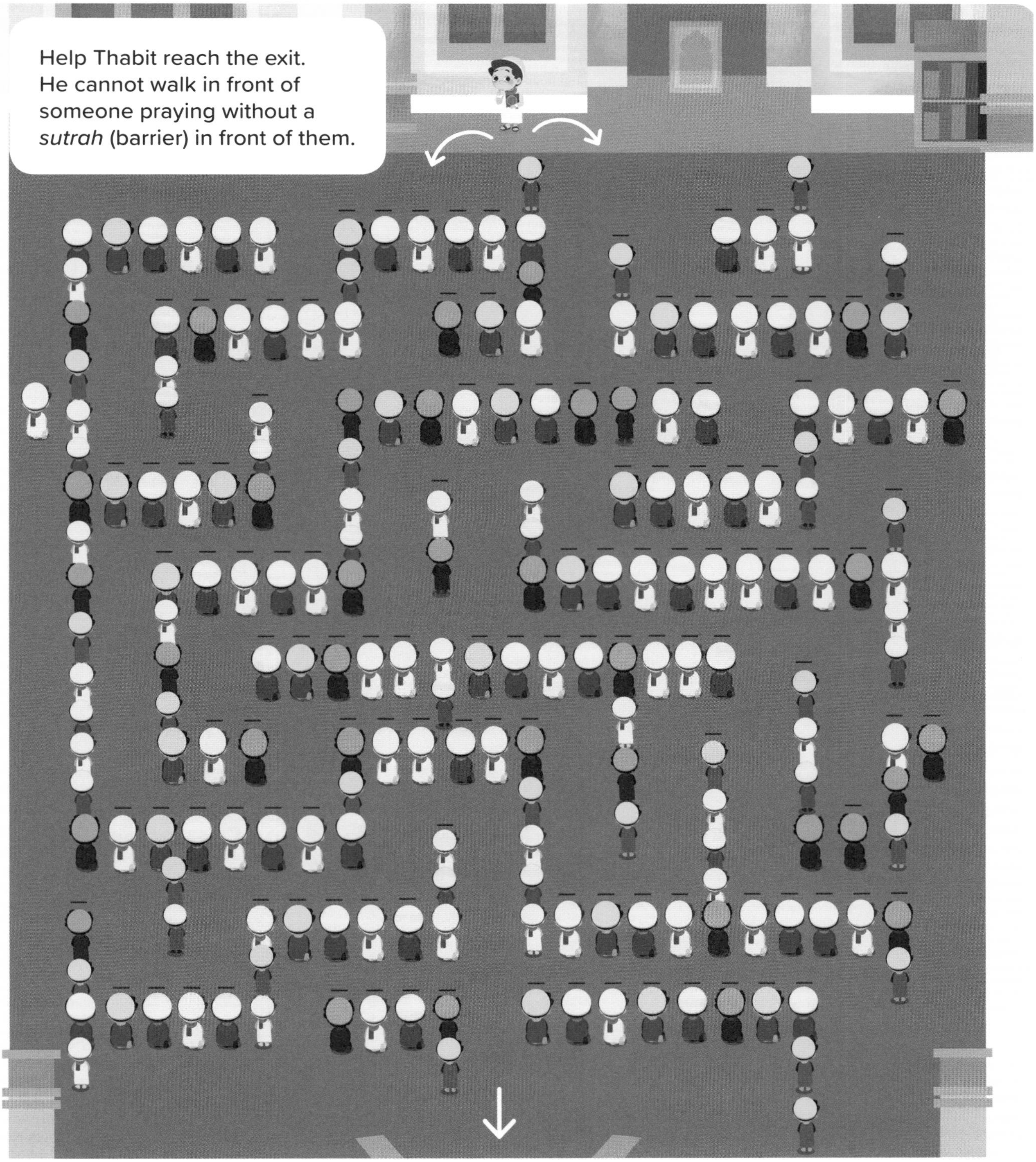

It All Adds Up

- Aisha has saved £500 and she wants to pay her zakah. Study the Help Box below and answer the questions that follow. You may need the help of a **grown-up** on this one!

Help Box

You pay Zakah if:

Your money is more than the *nisab* (about £232 today).

You've had the money for more than one year.

If so, you pay 2.5% of your money in zakah every year.

Use this space to work out your answers.

1. **Does Aisha have to pay zakah?**

   ....

2. **How much of her £500 does she need to give?**

   ....

3. **If Aisha uses the bank notes shown above to pay her Zakah, how much change will she have left?**

   ....

What Do You Hear?

- Which part of the Quran is each character reciting? Choose from the options given.

وَسِعَ كُرۡسِيُّهُ
ٱلسَّمَٰوَٰتِ وَٱلۡأَرۡضَ

- Surah Al-Ikhlas ◯
- Surah Al-Masad ◯
- Ayatul Kusri ◯

إِيَّاكَ نَعۡبُدُ
وَإِيَّاكَ نَسۡتَعِينُ

- Surah Al-Fatiha ◯
- Surah An-Naas ◯
- Surah Al-Falaq ◯

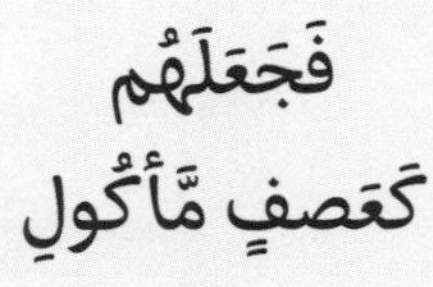

- Surah Al-Kawthar ◯
- Surah Al-Feel ◯
- Surah Al-Asr ◯

At Crossroads

- Complete the Ramadan crossword using the clues below.

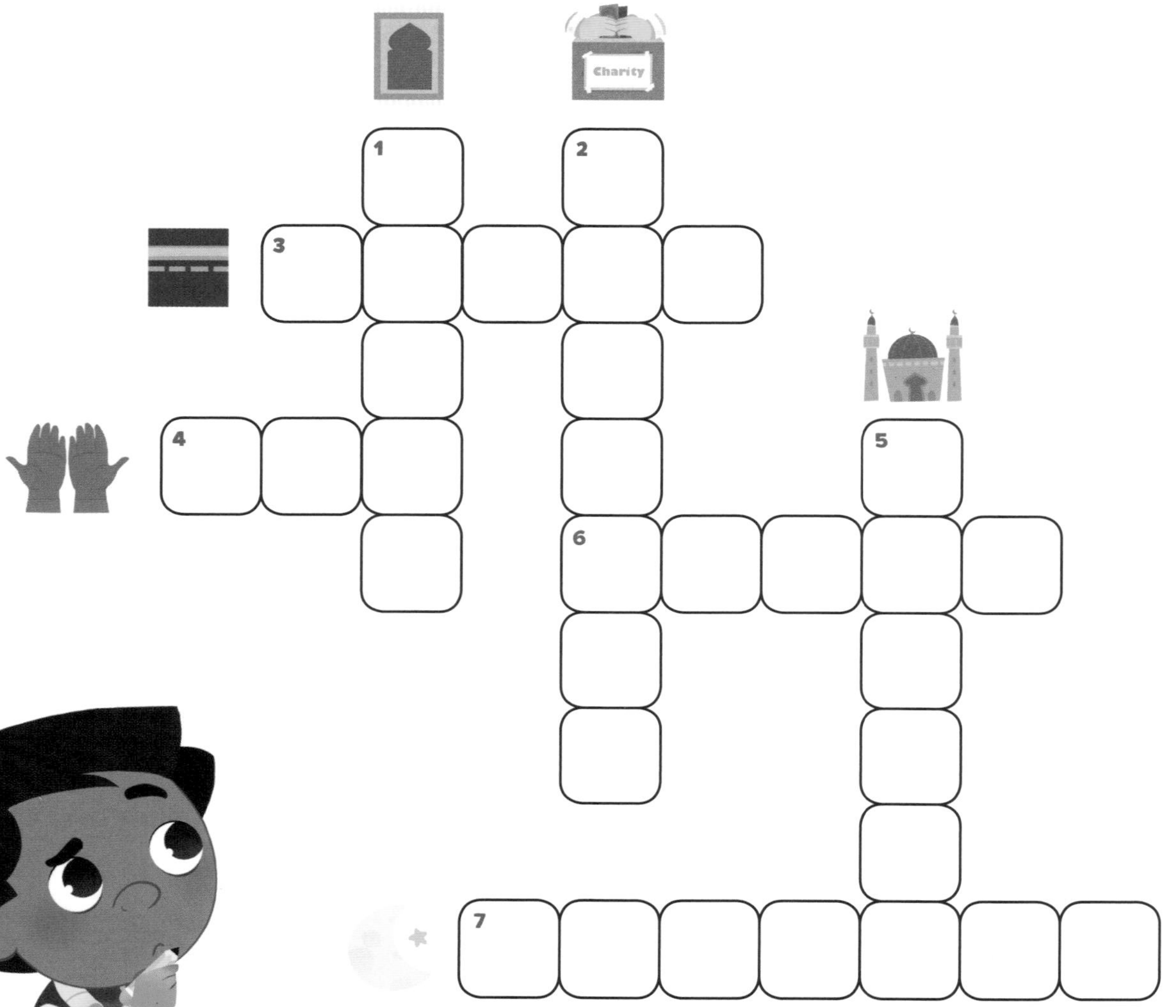

Clues

→ Across

3. Built by Ibrahim ﷺ
4. Ask Allah
6. Allah's Words
7. Month of Fasting

↓ Down

1. Prayer
2. Charity
5. A place to pray

That's Handy!

- Match the actions that should be done with the right hand, the left hand or both hands.

Holding Binoculars

Going to the Toilet

Eating

Shaking Hands

Touching the Quran

Carrying a Box

Skipping

Before You Fast

- Tick the circles for the characters who have a good enough reason to **not fast**.

I'm really poor, so I don't need to fast.

I'm feeling really unwell, so I'm not fasting today!

I'm travelling a long way today, so I won't be fasting.

Picture Perfect

- Paint this masjid following the colour code provided.

1 green
2 blue
3 grey
4 brown
5 yellow
6 dark blue
7 beige
8 violet

From the Heart

- Write down the top 3 *duas* that you plan to make this Ramadan and then write down what actions you will take as first steps.

ummah
dreams
health
hereafter
worship
parents
studies
friends
family
Jannah
home

1 Goal ....

Steps ....

2 Goal ....

Steps ....

3 Goal ....

Steps ....

You can be a legend too!

EXPLORE RAMADAN

Companion Code

- Cross out all of the letters that appear more than once. Use the remaining letters to spell the name of a Companion.

Z	R	ث	W	D	U	S	أ
E	ق	ص	ج	M	ق	O	Q
ص	T	G	ي	ج	ذ	E	Y
K	ذ	ة	P	P	I	ن	A
ظ	B	ث	ف	K	ك	ك	B
ل	R	W	I	م	H	C	أ
	ي	ل	V	O	D	و	Q
	C	و	ة	ظ	V	م	Y
	ن	S	ش	Z	X	ف	G
	ش	ز	N	ض	ز	X	ض

Re-arrange the letters after finding them.

....

....

Did you know that this Sahabi loved the Quran so much that he read it all in one night?

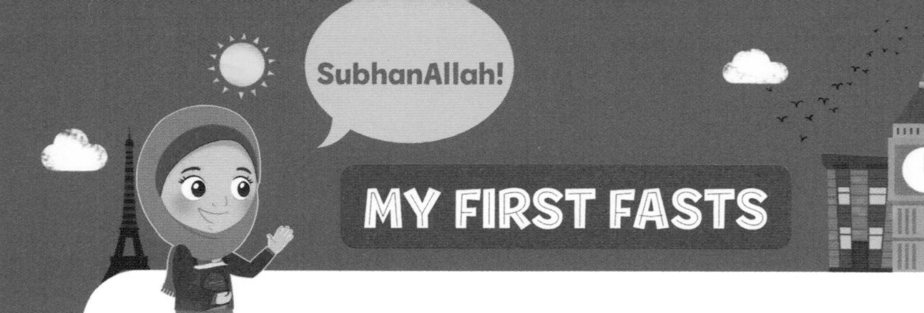

Excuse Me Please

- Cross-out the character that does not have a good excuse to miss fasting during Ramadan.

Qays' baby brother is just a young child!

Sofia has a mild cold.

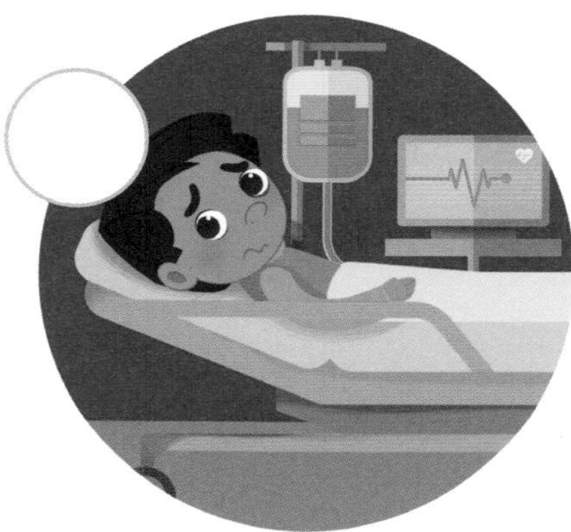

Layth had an accident, and is about to have an operation at the hospital.

Thabit's grandfather's kidneys are not working.

Sarah is travelling.

Sweet dreams!

58

GREAT DEEDS

Night Shield

- Read about the ways to protect yourself during the night, and list at least three points you can put in a checklist to do every night.

If you recite *Ayatul Kursi* before going to bed, Allah will send an Angel to protect you and naughty Shaytan will not be able to come close to you until the morning.

Going to sleep while you have wudu is an extra level of protection which can help you have sweet dreams.

The Prophet ﷺ used to dust-down his bed before lying down, just in case there was anything harmful on there.

There are lots of duas we can learn from the Prophet ﷺ about what to say before going to sleep, and it's a great time to cleanse your heart from any bad feelings about others.

My Bedtime Checklist

1. ....
2. ....
3. ....

Reaping Rewards

- Sofia's goals in Ramadan were to fast half of the month, memorise 6 *surahs* from the Quran and pray 20 extra prayers. Count the items below to see if she achieved her goals.

Fasts **Surahs** **Prayers**

The Best of Times

- Tick the moments that are some of the best times to make dua. Here's a clue: the best times are all linked to some kind of worship.

You've got this!

Crack the Code

- Starting with the letter marked by the arrow, move in a clock-wise direction and write down the letter that occurs every 6 spaces. Continue doing this until you pass the arrow point again. What does the message say?

....

....

Next-Level Fasting

- There's more to fasting than just not eating or drinking. Help Sofia label the start arrows with the level they lead to.

Level 1:
Staying away from food and drink.

Level 2:
Keeping your eyes, ears, tongue and hands away from all bad deeds.

Level 3:
Leaving everything that distracts you from Allah, by turning your heart to Allah and getting closer to Him.

You've got a big heart!

Quran Quiz

- Tick whether these statements are true or false. If they're false, correct them in the space provided.

	True	False	
The Quran was sent down in the month of Ramadan.	◯	◯	....
A Muslim should try to understand the meaning of the Quran and not just recite it.	◯	◯	....
The Quran has 42 'surahs'. (Look it up!)	◯	◯	....
The Quran was sent down in the night of Laylatul Qadr.	◯	◯	....
The Prophet ﷺ reviewed the Quran with the Angel Jibreel once every Ramadan.	◯	◯	....
You don't need wudu to touch the Quran.	◯	◯	....

Weather to Fast

- Muslims fast in all sorts of climates around the world. Place the **sticker** objects below the scene they belong to.

You've got a big heart!

GREAT DEEDS

Charity Clothes

- Sarah and Qays are giving their best clothes to charity. Using the key to help you, figure out which one of them is giving the most in value.

£4 £12 £10 £6 £7

£5 £3 £8

£4 £2 £3 £9

Sarah

Qays

....

....

....

....

Answer

....

Extra Fast

- Below are times when it's really good to fast. However, there's one mistake. Use the *hadeeth* to find it and cross it out.

Fridays

3 Middle Days of the Month

9 Days of Dhul-Hijjah

6 Fasts in Shawwal

Mondays & Thursdays

The Day of Ashura

The Day of Arafah

The Prophet ﷺ said:

" • *Fasting three days of every month (13th, 14th & 15th) is equal to Fasting a lifetime. (An-Nasaa'i)*

• *Fasting on the Day of 'Arafah wipes out the sins for two years: the previous year and the coming year, and fasting on 'Ashura, (10th Muharram) clears the sins of the previous year. (Muslim)*

• *Aisha (RA) narrates that the Prophet ﷺ was keen to fast on Mondays and Thursdays. (Tirmidhi)*

• *Whoever fasts Ramadan and follows it with six days of Shawwal, it will be as if he fasted for a lifetime. (Muslim)*

The Art of Prayer

- Complete the design of Aisha's prayer rug by repeating the patterns in each section.

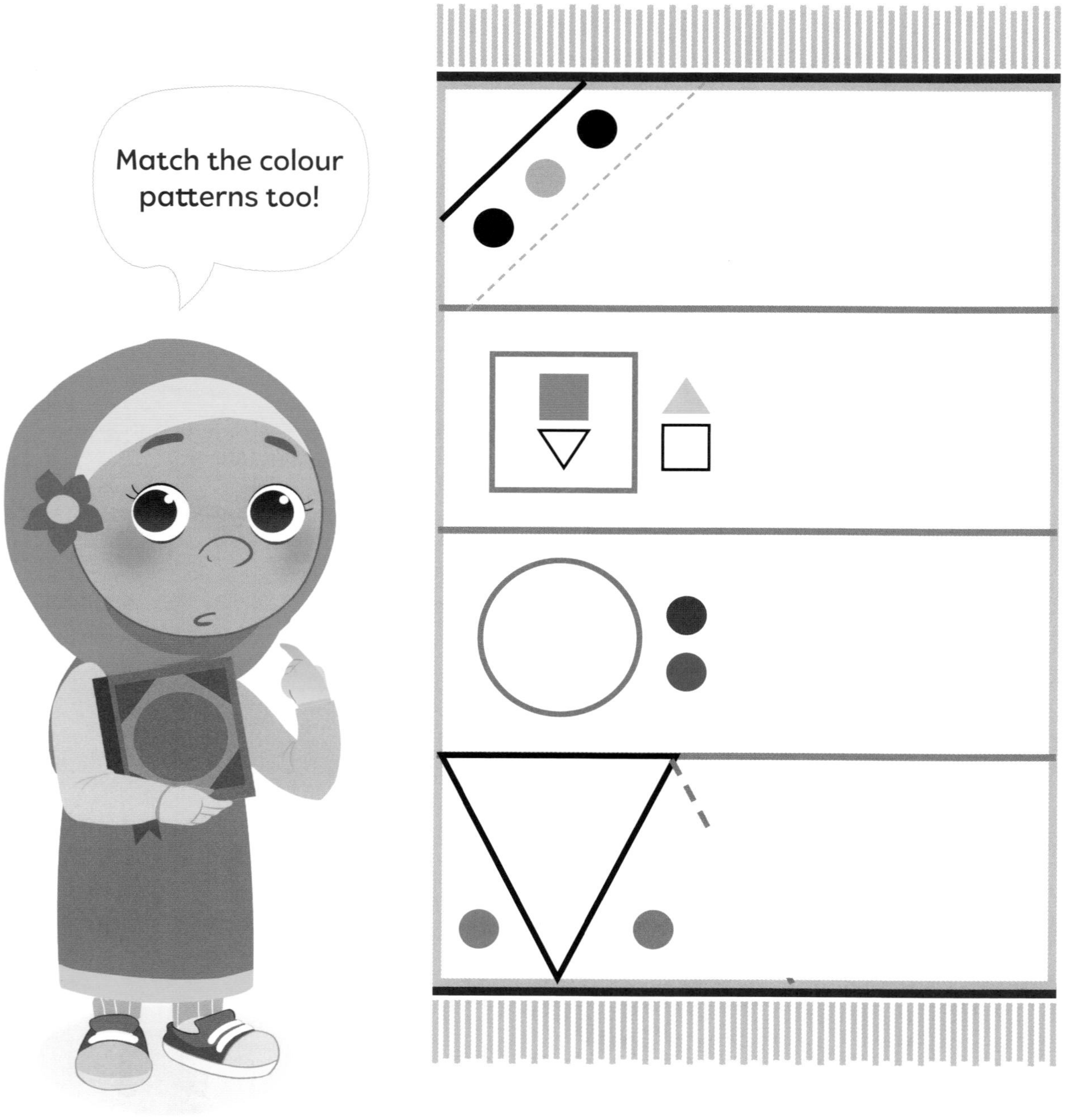

Match the colour patterns too!

Where Could it Be?

- Using **stickers**, pop the balloons that have a date that could be *Laylatul Qadr*. Use the *hadeeth* to help you.

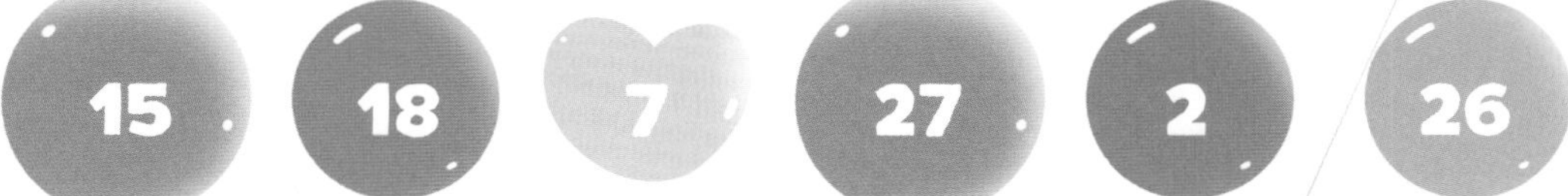

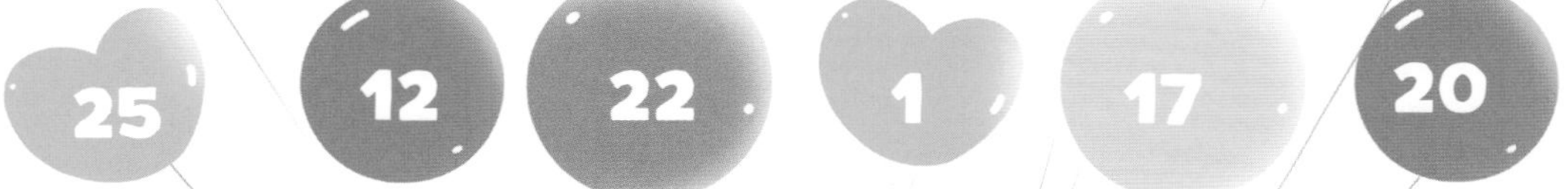

The Prophet ﷺ said:

❝ *Search for the Night of Qadr in the odd nights of the last ten days of Ramadan. (Bukhari)*

Now that's powerful!

Dua for a Powerful Night

- Using the key to help you, put the correct vowels on the letters to complete the dua for *Laylatul Qadr*.

Now you can memorise this dua too!

اللهم إنك عفو

تحب العفو

فاعف عني

اللهم إنك عفو

تحب العفو

فاعف عني

Vowels Key

ـِ	ـْ	ـٌّ	ـُّ	ـٰ	ـُ	ـَّ	ـَ
▬	⬢	✖	★	●	▲	◆	■

Nice and loud!

EID FUN

Takbeer!

- Using **stickers**, match the Arabic words of the Eid *Takbeer* to their correct translation, using the full meaning to help you.

اللّٰهُ أَكْبَرُ x3

لَا إِلٰهَ إِلَّا اللّٰهُ

وَاللّٰهُ أَكْبَرُ x3

وَلِلّٰهِ الْحَمْدُ

Meaning

Allah is the greatest.
Allah is the greatest.
Allah is the greatest.

There is no one worthy of worship (deity) except Allah.

And Allah is the greatest.
Allah is the greatest.
Allah is the greatest.

And to Allah belongs all praise.

Date Shake

- With the help of a grown-up, follow Layla's instructions to make this delicious date shake!

Ingredients

- 10 dates
- 250ml milk
- 1 small handful of ice cubes
- A pinch of ground cinnamon
- 1 tablespoon of honey (optional)
- 1 block of dark chocolate (optional for decoration)

Total Time:
10 minutes

1 Remove the seeds from the dates.

2 In a large blender, combine all the ingredients and blend for at least one minute, or until the mixture is smooth.

3 Pour into glasses, sprinkle some grated chocolate on top and serve with a straw.

Grown-ups!
Take a pic of your milkshake and share it using #ramadanlr You might be in for a surprise!

Have fun!

Eid Prayer Poster

- Follow the steps below to make your very own Eid prayer-times poster!

1 Cut out the Eid Prayer Poster from the cut-out section.

2 Using **stickers**, design the poster title and decorate the picture.

Jamat Times

Fajr: ....

1 .... 4 ....
2 .... 5 ....
3 .... 6 ....

3 With the help of a **grown-up** find out and write the Eid Jamat times at your local masjid on the poster.

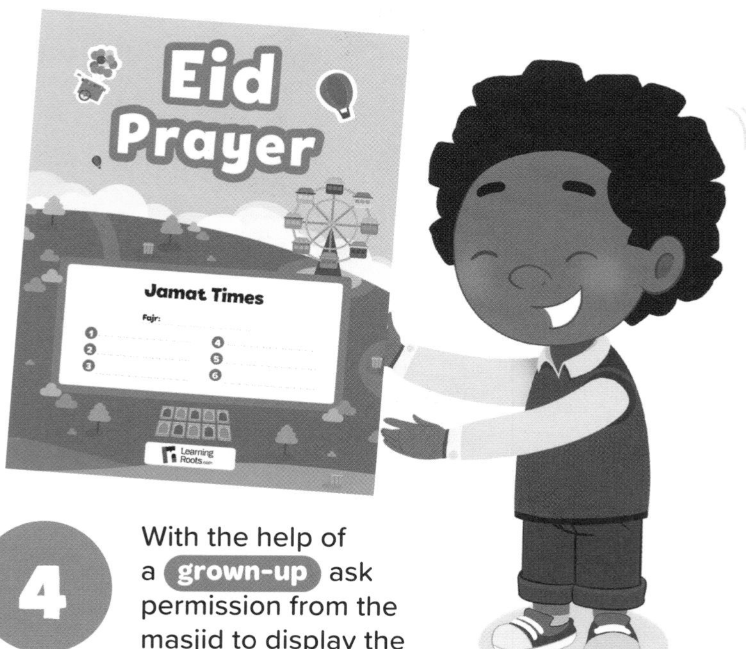

4 With the help of a **grown-up** ask permission from the masjid to display the poster for all to see!

So Nice to See You!

- Number each speech bubble to match it with the correct phrase. Then match each character with the meaning of the words they're saying.

1 **Assalamu 'Alaykum!**

2 **Eid Mubarak!**

3 **TaqabAllahu minna wa minkum!**

عيد مبارك

السلام عليكم

تقبل الله منا ومنكم

Peace be upon you!

May Allah accept (good deeds) from us and from you.

Have a blessed Eid!

Eid Cards & Games

- Play these fun tangram and matching games on Eid by following the steps below:

1. Cut out the tangram pieces from the cut-out section of this book. If you wish, you can mount the cut-outs on card beforehand.
2. Make the shapes of the minaret and prayer positions shown using the pieces you've cut out.

Eid Cards & Stickers

Cut out the Eid cards from the cut-out section and fold them in the middle. If you wish, you can mount the cut-outs on card beforehand. Fill in the cards and give them to your family and friends on Eid!

We've added some extra stickers outside of the orange frames in the stickers section for you to use as decoration on cards, envelopes or gifts on Eid day. Enjoy!

Joined Together

- Join the letters of the Arabic alphabet in order to help Hiba reveal the pattern she will sew on her Eid dress! Then answer the questions below.

ر ب ذ

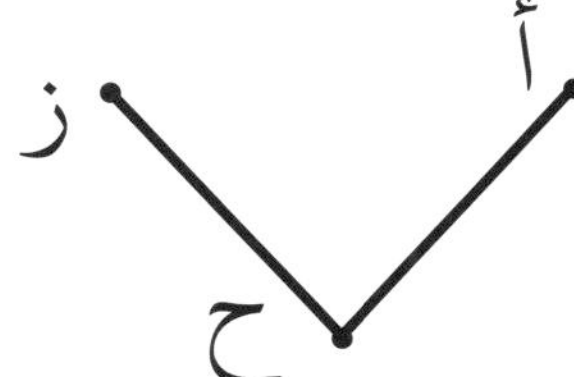

ج ت

د ث خ

1. **How many triangles are there in the pattern?** ....

2. **How many rhombuses can you spot?** ....

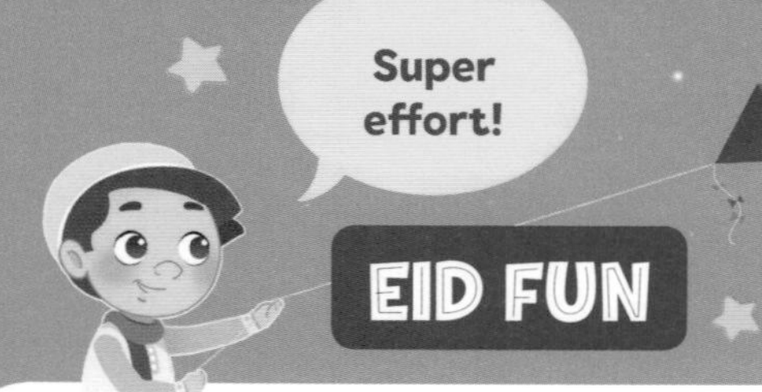

Super
effort!

Sudoku Dates

- Fill the table using **stickers**, making sure you get exactly one type of date in every column and row of the grid.

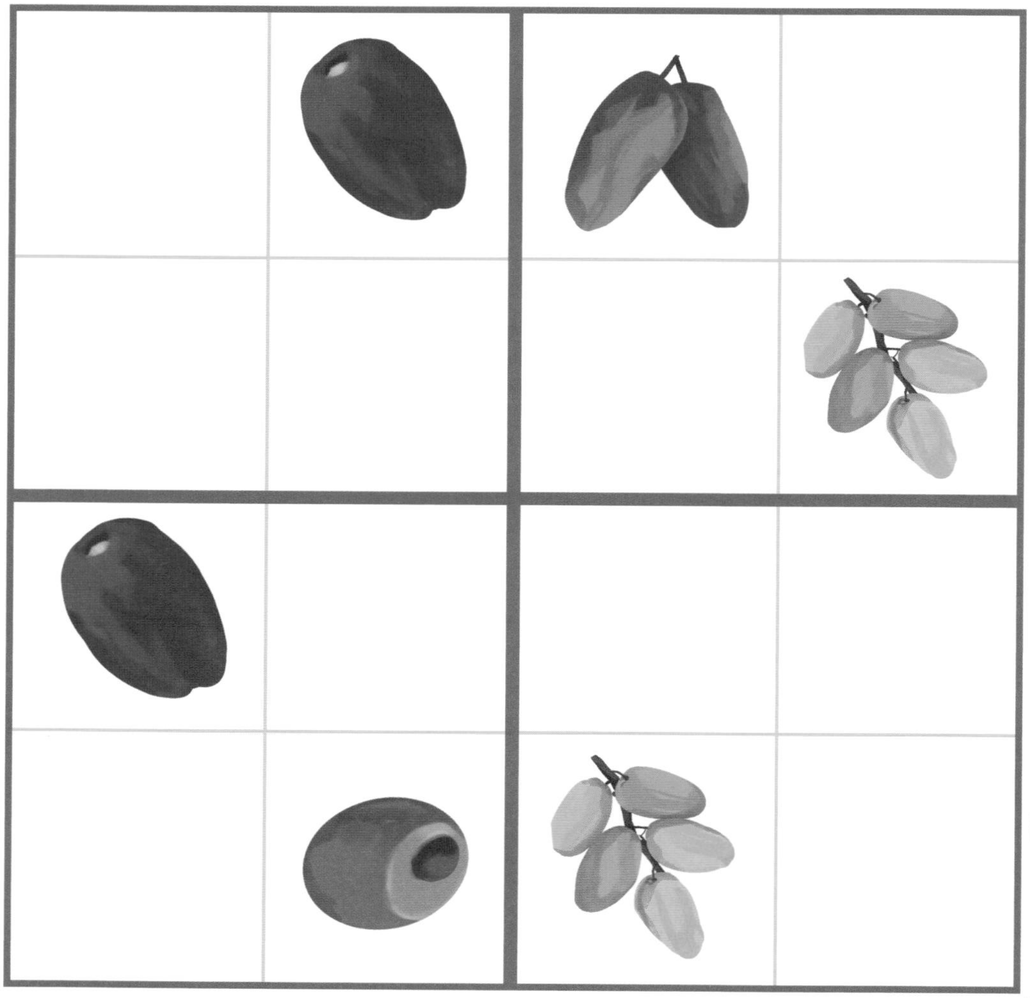

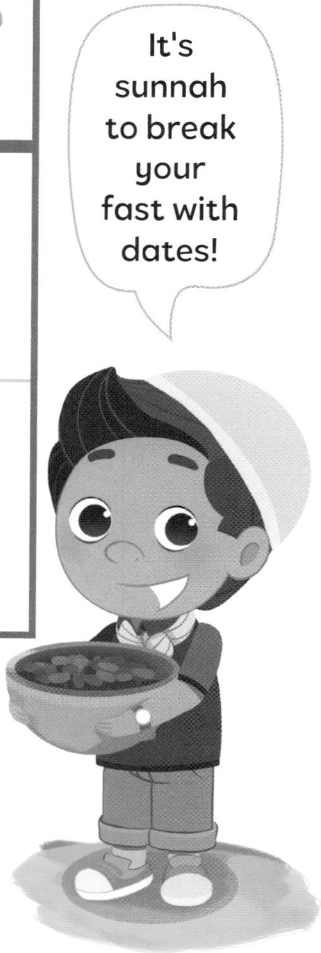
It's
sunnah
to break
your
fast with
dates!

ANSWERS

To see the answers
to the activities in this book,
please visit:

LearningRoots.com/Answers

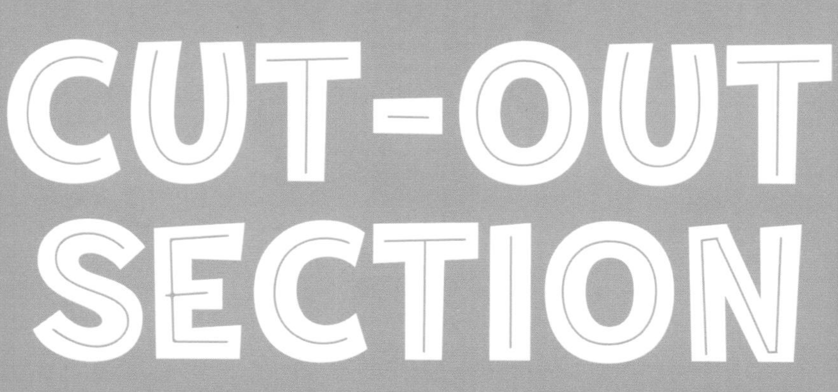
CUT-OUT
SECTION

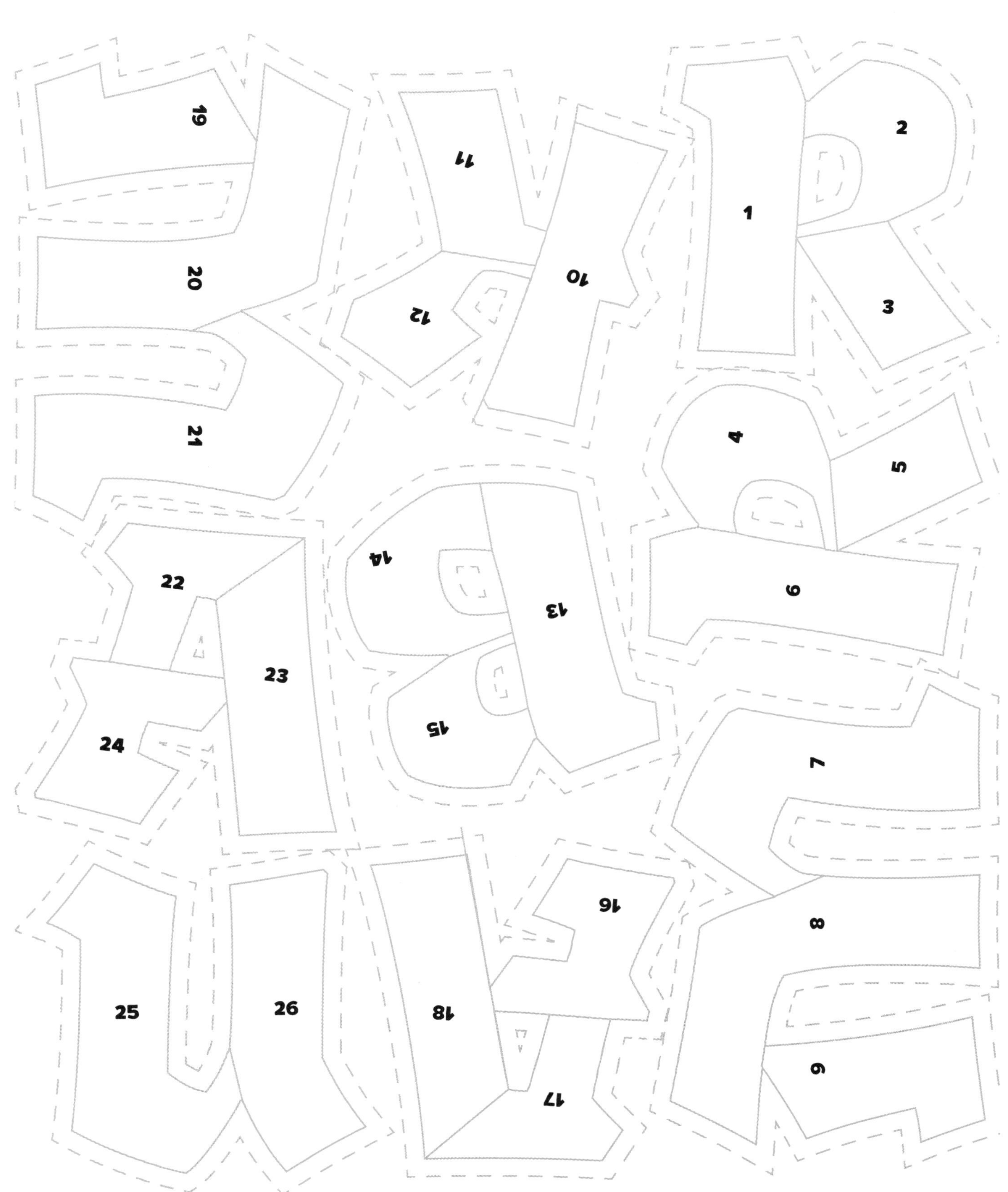
1
2
3
4
5
6
7
8
9
10
11
12
13
14
15
16
17
18
19
20
21
22
23
24
25
26

Learning Roots
Cut-Out Activity

Learning Roots
Cut-Out Activity

Learning Roots
Cut-Out Activity

Learning Roots
Cut-Out Activity

Learning Roots
Cut-Out Activity

Learning Roots
Cut-Out Activity

Learning Roots
Cut-Out Activity

Learning Roots
Cut-Out Activity

Learning Roots
Cut-Out Activity

Learning Roots
Cut-Out Activity

Learning Roots
Cut-Out Activity

Learning Roots
Cut-Out Activity

Learning Roots
Cut-Out Activity

Learning Roots
Cut-Out Activity

Learning Roots
Cut-Out Activity

Learning Roots
Cut-Out Activity

Learning Roots
Cut-Out Activity

Learning Roots
Cut-Out Activity

Learning Roots
Cut-Out Activity

Learning Roots
Cut-Out Activity

Learning Roots
Cut-Out Activity

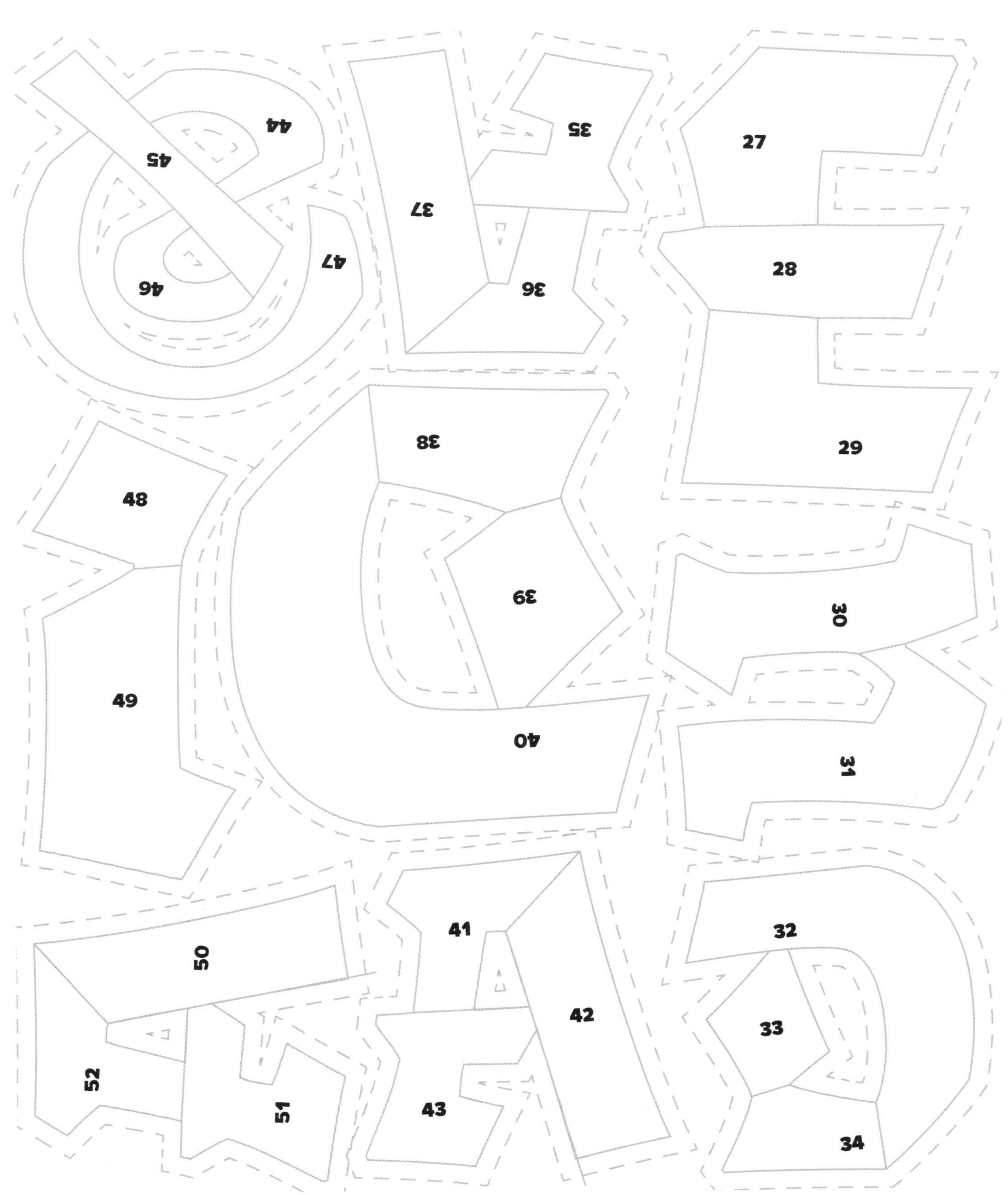
44
45
35
27
37
47
46
36
28
38
29
48
39
30
49
40
31
41
32
50
42
33
52
51
43
34

Learning Roots
Cut-Out Activity

Learning Roots
Cut-Out Activity

Learning Roots
Cut-Out Activity

Learning Roots
Cut-Out Activity

Learning Roots
Cut-Out Activity

Learning Roots
Cut-Out Activity

Learning Roots
Cut-Out Activity

Learning Roots
Cut-Out Activity

Learning Roots
Cut-Out Activity

Learning Roots
Cut-Out Activity

Learning Roots
Cut-Out Activity

Learning Roots
Cut-Out Activity

Learning Roots
Cut-Out Activity

Learning Roots
Cut-Out Activity

Learning Roots
Cut-Out Activity

Learning Roots
Cut-Out Activity

Learning Roots
Cut-Out Activity

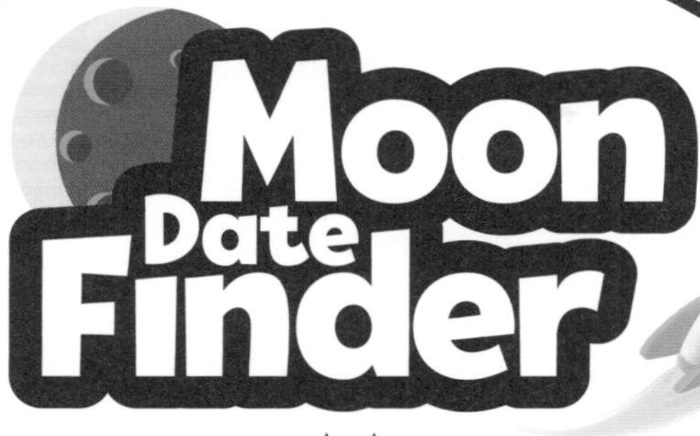

Spin the wheel and discover the dates of the lunar month by mathcing the phases of the moon.

The number in the red circle tells you the lunar date!

1 New Moon

3 Waxing Crescent

8 First Quarter

10 Waxing Gibbous

15 Full Moon

20 Waning Gibbous

24 Last Quarter

27 Waning Crescent

Learning Roots
Cut-Out Activity

Learning Roots
Cut-Out Activity

Learning Roots
Cut-Out Activity

Learning Roots
Cut-Out Activity

Learning Roots
Cut-Out Activity

Learning Roots
Cut-Out Activity

Learning Roots
Cut-Out Activity

Learning Roots
Cut-Out Activity

Learning Roots
Cut-Out Activity

Learning Roots
Cut-Out Activity

Learning Roots
Cut-Out Activity

Learning Roots
Cut-Out Activity

Learning Roots
Cut-Out Activity

Learning Roots
Cut-Out Activity

Learning Roots
Cut-Out Activity

Learning Roots
Cut-Out Activity

Learning Roots
Cut-Out Activity

Learning Roots
Cut-Out Activity

Learning Roots
Cut-Out Activity

Learning Roots
Cut-Out Activity

Learning Roots
Cut-Out Activity

Breaking Your Fast

ذَهَبَ الظَّمَأُ، وَابْتَلَّتِ
العُرُوقُ، وَثَبَتَ الأَجْرُ
إِنْ شَاءَ اللَّهُ

Thahaba ath-thama oo wabtallatil-'urooqu, wathabatal ajru in-sha-Allah.

The thirst has gone and the veins are moist, and the reward is assured, if Allah wills.

ABU DAWOOD

Learning Roots.com

Learning Roots
Cut-Out Activity

Learning Roots
Cut-Out Activity

Learning Roots
Cut-Out Activity

Learning Roots
Cut-Out Activity

Learning Roots
Cut-Out Activity

Learning Roots
Cut-Out Activity

Learning Roots
Cut-Out Activity

Learning Roots
Cut-Out Activity

Learning Roots
Cut-Out Activity

Learning Roots
Cut-Out Activity

Learning Roots
Cut-Out Activity

Learning Roots
Cut-Out Activity

Learning Roots
Cut-Out Activity

Learning Roots
Cut-Out Activity

Learning Roots
Cut-Out Activity

Learning Roots
Cut-Out Activity

Learning Roots
Cut-Out Activity

On Laylatul Qadr

اَللَّهُمَّ إِنَّكَ عَفُوٌّ،
تُحِبُّ الْعَفْوَ
فَاعْفُ عَنِّي

Allahumma innaka ‘afuwwun,
tuhibbul-‘afwa, fa’fu ‘anni

O Allah! You are Most Forgiving, and You love forgiveness, so forgive me!

AT-TIRMIDHI

Learning Roots.com

Learning Roots
Cut-Out Activity

Learning Roots
Cut-Out Activity

Learning Roots
Cut-Out Activity

Learning Roots
Cut-Out Activity

Learning Roots
Cut-Out Activity

Learning Roots
Cut-Out Activity

Learning Roots
Cut-Out Activity

Learning Roots
Cut-Out Activity

Learning Roots
Cut-Out Activity

Learning Roots
Cut-Out Activity

Learning Roots
Cut-Out Activity

Learning Roots
Cut-Out Activity

Learning Roots
Cut-Out Activity

Learning Roots
Cut-Out Activity

Learning Roots
Cut-Out Activity

Learning Roots
Cut-Out Activity

Learning Roots
Cut-Out Activity

Learning Roots
Cut-Out Activity

Learning Roots
Cut-Out Activity

Learning Roots
Cut-Out Activity

Learning Roots
Cut-Out Activity

Jamat Times

Fajr: ....

1 ....

2 ....

3 ....

4 ....

5 ....

6 ....

Name of Centre

Prepared by

Learning Roots
Cut-Out Activity

Learning Roots
Cut-Out Activity

Learning Roots
Cut-Out Activity

Learning Roots
Cut-Out Activity

Learning Roots
Cut-Out Activity

Learning Roots
Cut-Out Activity

Learning Roots
Cut-Out Activity

Learning Roots
Cut-Out Activity

Learning Roots
Cut-Out Activity

Learning Roots
Cut-Out Activity

Learning Roots
Cut-Out Activity

Learning Roots
Cut-Out Activity

Learning Roots
Cut-Out Activity

Learning Roots
Cut-Out Activity

Learning Roots
Cut-Out Activity

Learning Roots
Cut-Out Activity

Learning Roots
Cut-Out Activity

Learning Roots
Cut-Out Activity

Learning Roots
Cut-Out Activity

Learning Roots
Cut-Out Activity

Learning Roots
Cut-Out Activity

- Cut the pieces out and then make the shapes shown below. What does each shape show?

Make these shapes using the pieces you've cut out.

Learning Roots
Cut-Out Activity

Learning Roots
Cut-Out Activity

Learning Roots
Cut-Out Activity

Learning Roots
Cut-Out Activity

Learning Roots
Cut-Out Activity

Learning Roots
Cut-Out Activity

Learning Roots
Cut-Out Activity

Learning Roots
Cut-Out Activity

Learning Roots
Cut-Out Activity

Learning Roots
Cut-Out Activity

Learning Roots
Cut-Out Activity

Learning Roots
Cut-Out Activity

Learning Roots
Cut-Out Activity

Learning Roots
Cut-Out Activity

Learning Roots
Cut-Out Activity

Learning Roots
Cut-Out Activity

Learning Roots
Cut-Out Activity

Eid Mubarak

Learning
Roots.com

Eid Mubarak

Learning
Roots.com

Wishing you an accepted Ramadan and a blessed Eid!

Wishing you an accepted Ramadan and a blessed Eid!

STICKERS SECTION

FEEDBACK PLEASE!

We would love to hear your thoughts on this book. Please let us know at:

LearningRoots.com/Feedback

STICKERS

Activity 1

Qays
Aisha
Thabit
Hiba
Zayd
Sofia
Layth
Sarah

Activity 8

Activity 13

Alhamdulillah

Bismillah

Maghrib Athan

Dua for Breaking Fast

Activity 68

Activity 17

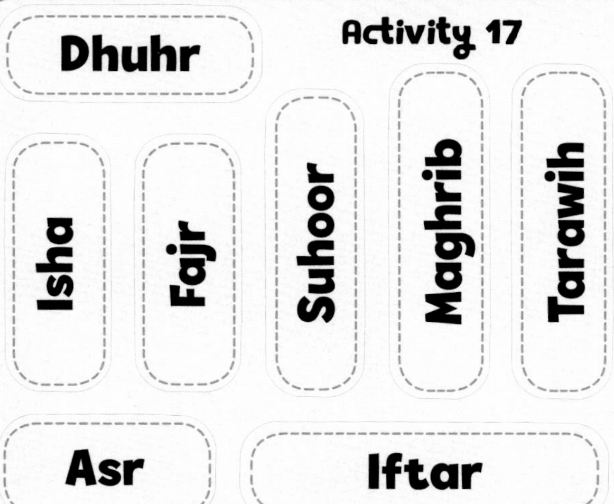

Activity 70

greatest
all praise
No
Allah
Allah
except
and for Allah
deity

Activity 31

Activity 4

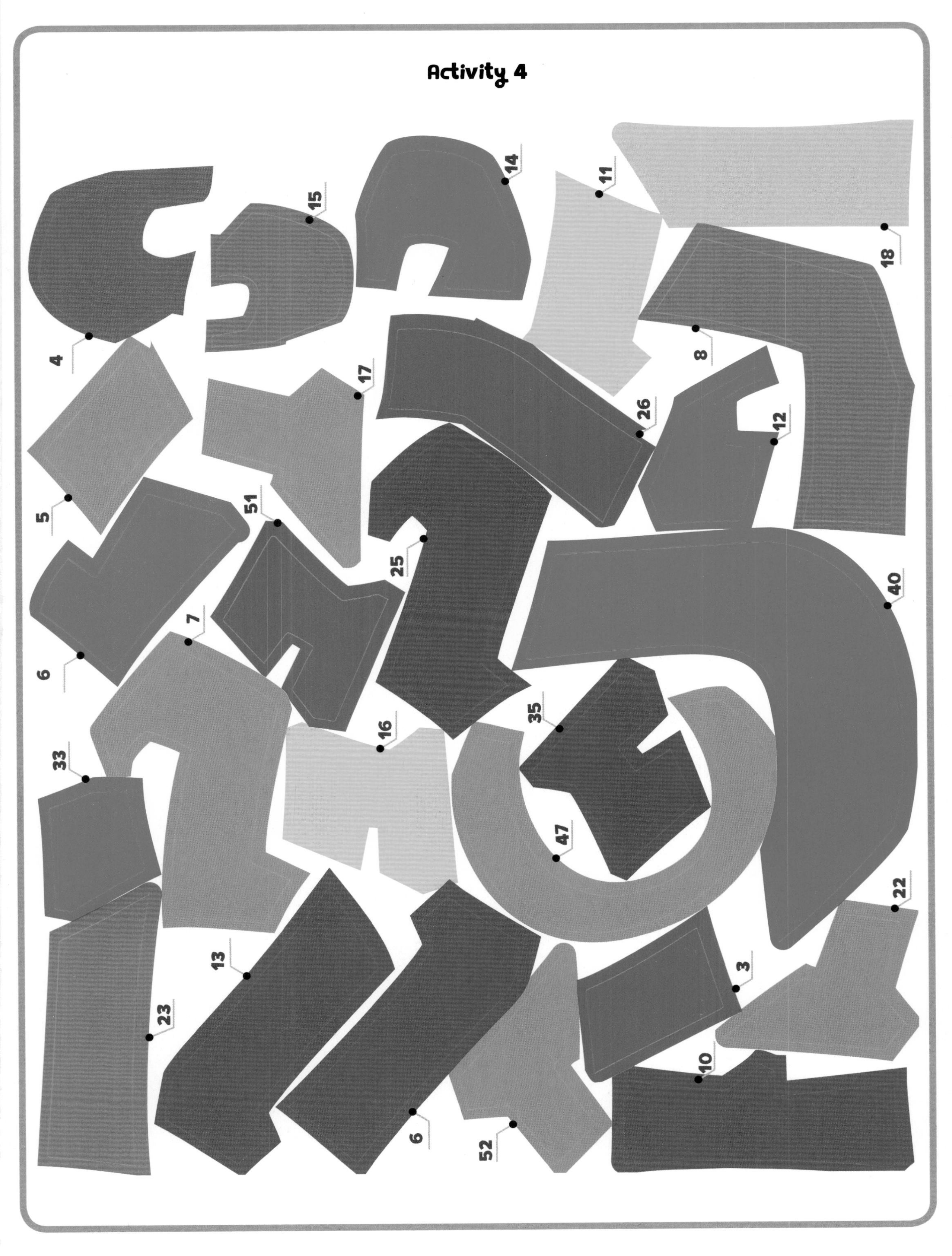

Activity 4

19
39
49
24
27
36
30
48
41
32
28
2
1
37
44
29
31
45
43
46
34
42
38
20
21
50

Activity 72
E d y r p i
r a e

EID
Mubarak

EID
Mubarak

EID
Mubarak

EID
Mubarak

Activity 76

EID
Mubarak

EID
Mubarak

EID
Mubarak

Activity 64

EID
Mubarak

Activity 3

1 2 3 4 5 6 7 8 9

10 11 12 13 14 15 16 17 18

19 20 21 22 23 24 25 26 27

28 29 30 1 4 4 0 1 2 3

1 2 3 4 5 6 7 8 9 10 11 12 13

14 15 16 17 18 19 20 21 22 23 24 25 26

27 28 29 30 31 2 0 1 9 2 0 2 1